Mosdos Press Literature

OPAL

DAISY
2

Educators transmitting appropriate values and academic excellence

Mosdos Press

Mosdos Press
Cleveland, Ohio

Educators transmitting appropriate values and academic excellence

Mosdos Press

Part Two
ISBN-10: 0-9858078-4-9
ISBN-13: 978-0-985-80784-9

Set
ISBN-10: 0-9858078-3-0
ISBN-13: 978-0-985-80783-2

Mosdos Press
Literature

EDITOR-IN-CHIEF
Judith Factor

CREATIVE/ART DIRECTOR
Carla Martin

SENIOR CURRICULUM WRITER
Abigail Rozen

COPY EDITOR
Laya Dewick

WRITERS
Lessons in Literature / Jill's Journals:
Jill Brotman

Author Biographies:
Aliza B. Ganchrow

TEXT AND CURRICULUM ADVISOR
Rabbi Ahron Dovid Goldberg

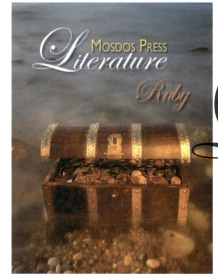

MOSDOS PRESS
Literature

ANTHOLOGY SERIES

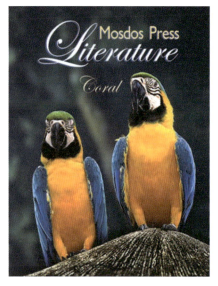

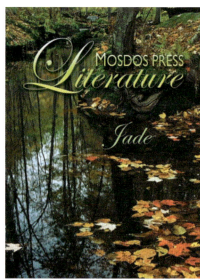

OPAL

RUBY

CORAL

PEARL

JADE

GOLD

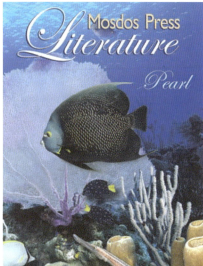

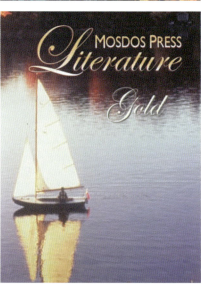

unit 4

all about setting!

unit 5

all about theme!

unit 6

the grand finalé!

unit 4

A MOUSE HOUSE

SMALL TOWN AMERICA

CHANGE

all about setting!

THE HEARTLAND

AMASINA, DOCTOR OF THE AMAZON

MORE ABOUT SETTING

- **Setting** is the background of a story.
- Setting tells us *when* and *where* a story takes place.
- Some stories or poems are mainly about setting and do not have a strong plot or exciting characters.
- For this type of story in particular, it is very important to *visualize*, or picture in your mind, the setting being described.

THINK ABOUT IT!

1. Why had the American doctors come to the rain forest?
2. Describe the trees of the rain forest.
3. Who are the Trio and what do they eat?

Amasina was very pleased. The American doctors had decided to teach him how to carry out medical treatments used in the United States. They were also going to give him simple medical instruments and medications. He would be able to help the people of his tribe by giving injections, fluids, and antibiotics. Amasina would assist the doctors in return. He would share his knowledge about plants of the Amazon that he used to treat wounds and disease.

The American doctors had come to the tropical rain forests to help the people of his tribe with their health care. They had been amazed by Amasina's knowledge of the Amazon plants that could be used for medicine. These plants could be used for both tropical diseases and for diseases found in the United States and Europe. Amasina knew about all of these plants.

When Amasina was growing up, both his mother and his father taught him about the many special plants. Amasina was now 68. He had learned so much, he was able to identify 1,300 plants that could be used to treat disease. Many of these plants are used in different combinations, so teaching the Americans what he knew would take a lot of time.

The Amazon is home to more species of plants and animals than any other place on Earth. The rain forest is very beautiful, because the plants are so lush. Tropical rain forests contain big, tall trees. Some are taller than 230 feet. Their branches overlap and form a covering. This roof created by the tree branches is full of animal and plant life.

There are many kinds of animals and birds found in the rain forest. There are also many snakes, frogs, fish, and insects. The insects are important to the rain forest. Some of the insects, however, can carry diseases that affect human beings. The many tribal people who live in the Amazon can be infected with these diseases. Fortunately, Amasina's knowledge helps him cure everything from snakebites to tumors. It is wonderful that Amasina can be such a help to his tribe.

Amasina's tribe is called the Trio. They grow cassava, bananas, and rice. With these starchy basic foods, they eat fish and game taken from surrounding rivers and forests. Besides medicinal plants, the forest provides them with building materials and dyes.

An organization called the Amazon Conservation Team (ACT) has been helping women and men like Amasina to train apprentices, so that their knowledge will be passed on. An apprentice is someone who learns an art or a science by practicing for several years with an expert. Amasina is teaching three apprentices how to prepare medicines and use healing plants.

Amasina chooses his apprentices based on trust. He says he looks at the relationship between young persons and their parents. He also looks at how they get along in the tribal community. He has two apprentices in the program and is also teaching his son. Amasina and his apprentices work in one of the two clinics about five days a week.

Many untold treasures await discovery with the medicinal plants used by the doctors of the rain forest tribes. More than 100 pharmaceutical companies and even the U.S. government are now paying for projects that study the knowledge of these doctors and the specific plants they use.

Blueprint for Reading

INTO . . . *The Town That Moved*

When a town calls itself "a town on the move," it usually means that the town is growing in size. When we talk about the town of Hibbing, Minnesota, though, we are talking about a town that actually moved! It was not just the people who moved, it was the buildings that moved. The hotel, the school, the shops, and the houses were all put on logs and rolled to another location! Why? You will find out as you read *The Town That Moved*.

EYES ON — *When the Plot is About the Setting*

In many stories, the setting is only the background of the story; it is the plot that we are really interested in. For example, in a story about a king, a castle might be the setting. The castle is important, but it is not the most important part of the story—the story is about the king. In some stories, however, the plot is actually *about* the setting. In *The Town That Moved,* the setting is the town of Hibbing in the state of Minnesota. The story is *about* the setting—the town of Hibbing! As you read *The Town That Moved*, try to visualize Hibbing as it started, as it grew, and as it was moved to a new location.

The Town That Moved

Mary Jane Finsand

Once upon a time, when the United States was still a young nation, much of the country was wilderness.

And so it was in northern Minnesota.

What was there? Forests and lakes. Bears and deer and wolves.

Some men thought there might even be gold and silver. They were not sure, but they were curious. So they went to the wilderness to seek their fortunes.

Some of these men came to hunt the animals. Then they sold the furs to people in cities far away. Others came to cut down trees and sell the lumber.

Still other men came to look for silver or gold. They did not find much of either in northern Minnesota. They did not have an easy life either!

There were no towns. There were no roads. The winters were long and cold. It was no place to bring a family. The men had to come by themselves.

Then, in August of 1891, a cyclone blew over the wilderness. The winds were fast and strong. They blew down many great trees.

Underneath, on the roots of the trees and in the holes they left behind, men discovered iron ore! There may not have been gold in northern Minnesota, but in the 1800s iron ore was almost as exciting.

Iron ore is the rock from which we get iron. In the 1800s iron was badly needed to build railroad trains and tracks.

It wasn't long before news of the iron ore in Minnesota had spread all around the country. Men began to pour into Minnesota. They came to start iron ore mines.

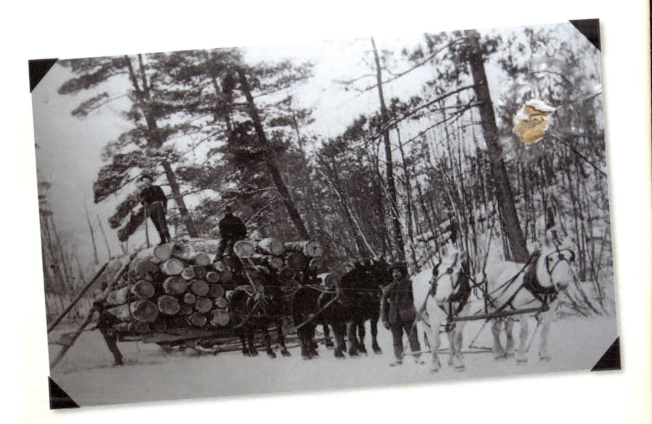

Some men came to cut down trees and sell the lumber

One of those men was named Frank Hibbing. Frank Hibbing knew that if he started an iron ore mine he would need many men to work in it. The men would want to bring their families. So Hibbing decided to build a town.

First he bought land. Then he hired men to build roads. He hired other men to build log cabins for the families.

Soon people were coming from all over the country to work in Hibbing's mine and live in his town. People even came from countries far away like Ireland, Sweden, and

People even came from Ireland, Sweden, and Germany

Germany. Many came to work in the mine, but others came to open stores. Soon there were schools and houses of worship and banks, too.

On August 15, 1893, the people voted to become the town of Hibbing, Minnesota. Hibbing became famous for its rich iron ore. The town grew and grew. Everyone who lived there was very proud of Hibbing. They wanted to make it a beautiful city.

They built fancy theaters and lovely parks and fine houses. They started excellent schools for their children, and they took wonderful care of their town.

Then one day the mine owners made a discovery: THE VERY BEST IRON ORE WAS RIGHT BENEATH THE TOWN OF HIBBING!

The people of Hibbing would have to move. If they didn't, the mines would have to shut down. The miners would be out of work. Soon the other businesses would have to close down, too.

The people of Hibbing were very upset. They had worked so hard to build their beautiful town. How could they leave it? How could they watch it be torn down to make way for new mines?

"Where will we go?" they asked.

"We will build you a new town," said the mine owners.

"But what about our fine homes and our fancy theaters and our beautiful hotels?" the people asked.

The mine owners thought and thought, and finally they came up with a solution.

"We will move your homes!" they said. "We will move the whole town!"

It sounded like a wonderful idea. But how on earth would they do it?

The mine owners and the people sat down together to think and talk.

"We have horses and tractors," said one man. "Maybe we could pull the buildings."

"But we can't pull big buildings along the ground," said the mayor. "They will break into pieces. We need wheels or something."

"Wheels are a problem," said the mine owners. "Most of our wheels are just not large or strong enough to move a building."

"Well," said someone else, "we certainly have lots of trees. We could cut them down, then make them smooth, and roll our houses on them."

"That's it!" everyone cried.

So the mine owners and the people began to get ready for moving day. They separated all the buildings from their basements. Then they dug new basements for all those buildings. They chopped down trees. Then they cut away the branches. They made the logs smooth.

People all over the world heard about Hibbing's plan to move.

"Impossible!" they said.

One big city newspaper wrote: "HIBBING GONE CRAZY!"

No one believed that the people of Hibbing could move their whole town.

Finally moving day arrived. The Hibbing Hotel would be the first building moved. The miners attached large chains and ropes to cranes from the mine. The cranes would be powered by steam engines. Then the chains were wrapped over and under the Hibbing Hotel. Slowly the cranes lifted the hotel. Then they swung it over and lowered it gently onto a log roller.

Hibbing
Gone
Crazy!

Next ropes and straps were wrapped around the hotel, then attached to horses up front. "Giddap! Giddap!" shouted the drivers. The horses started forward. Slowly the Hibbing Hotel rolled down the street.

As soon as the back log rolled out from under the building, people grabbed it. They strapped it to a horse and pulled it up to the front. Then they slid it underneath again.

Down the street the buildings rolled to their new locations. Day in and day out the people of Hibbing worked to save their beautiful town.

At last all the business buildings had been moved. Next would come the houses.

"What should we do with our furniture?" the women asked.

"And our toys and clothes," said the children.

"Leave everything in the houses," they were told. "And you can ride in your houses, too."

The very next day the first house was lifted onto logs. Down the street it came. A log was placed up front. Then a log rolled out back. That log was placed up front, and another log rolled out back.

And so it went until, one after another, 186 houses had been moved. The people of Hibbing had done it! They had moved their whole town!

Hibbing's move began in the year 1912, but the major push didn't come until 1921, and most of the buildings were moved in the 1920s. It wasn't until the fall of 1953 or the spring of 1954, though, that the very last building was finally moved.

The people of Hibbing moved their town because they loved it. It wasn't until many years later that they found they had made history. If you go to Hibbing today you can see many of the buildings that were rolled on logs to where they now stand. And people are still proud to say, "We are from Hibbing, the town that moved!"

About the Author

Mary Jane Finsand has written one children's book and many cookbooks. In her story for children, she wanted to help children learn about the unusual story of the town of Hibbing. In her cookbooks, she is particularly interested in providing recipes that people with diabetes can eat without compromising on taste.

Snail's Pace

Aileen L. Fisher

Maybe it's so
that snails are slow:
they trudge along and tarry.

But isn't it true
you'd slow up, too,
if you had a house to carry?

Studying the Selection

FIRST IMPRESSIONS

The early settlers arrived in America and found nothing but wilderness. Do you wonder how the country grew to have so many towns and cities in so short a time?

QUICK REVIEW

1. Why was iron ore so valuable during the late 1800s?
2. What did Frank Hibbing do to make sure that men would come to the wilderness to work in his mine?
3. What discovery was made that changed everything for the people of Hibbing?
4. What decision was made that would save the town?

FOCUS

5. Frank Hibbing was a man who had just the qualities it takes to build something from scratch. For example, he was not afraid to try something new. In two sentences, write about one other quality that made Frank Hibbing a successful builder and leader.
6. *The Town That Moved* has four settings. What are they?

CREATING AND WRITING

7. To persuade people to settle the American frontier, fliers were often written and distributed wherever people lived. After all, the frontier was dangerous, wild, and unfamiliar. The fliers had to present good reasons why people should come. Imagine that you are Frank Hibbing and you want to attract people to your new town in Minnesota. Write and illustrate a flier to be distributed in some American towns, inviting the residents to work for you and live in Hibbing.
8. Your class will pretend they are a group of Americans who live in a small settlement. Frank Hibbing has sent fliers out encouraging people to leave their homes and come to Hibbing. The settlers want to make the decision together. Either they will all go or they will all stay. The teacher will choose six students to speak. Three will speak in favor of moving to Hibbing and three will speak against moving. When all six students have spoken, the class will vote on moving to Hibbing or staying put.

Jill's Journal:

On Assignment in Bankhead, Canada

When I first learned that people moved whole houses and buildings, I could not believe it. Even if I could have believed it, I couldn't have imagined it. Even when I was told how it was done, it just didn't seem possible to me. But, facts are facts, and when I finally visited an entire town that was about to move, I became a believer! The town was Bankhead, in Alberta, Canada.

It is 1922, and I am in Bankhead. I am visiting with the Orner family. I have helped Mrs. Orner with some of the cooking—not so easy in a big cast iron pot over the hearth—so she has taken time from her chores to go for a walk with me. You cannot imagine how beautiful it is here! I see hundreds of tall trees and magnificent mountains in the distance.

Mrs. Orner tells me that the town was founded in 1903 by the Canadian Pacific Railway. "The Canadian Pacific Railway needed coal to power its steam locomotives. To attract miners and their families, they built homes and created an entire town for the men who would work in the nearby Pacific Coal mines. They named the town Bankhead. The miners rented their homes from the railway company."

I ask her how many miners there are. "Well, maybe 200 or 300."

She goes on to explain, "My husband is one of the miners. He works hard! We have three little ones and want them to have a good life. I'm not sure whether

MOVE 38 HOUSES 6 MILES 40 DAYS

Bankhead Village Being Moved to Banff by Calgary Contractor

(Special to The Herald)

BANFF, March 23.—Thirty-eight houses moved six and one-half miles in 40 days, over difficult mountain roads, from Bankhead to Banff, is the record established to date by Chas. Riddock, house-mover, of Calgary.

◆ ◆ ◆

Excerpt from The Calgary Herald

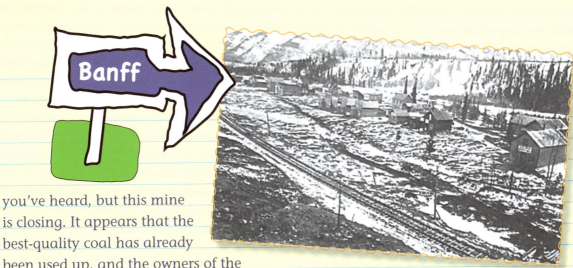

you've heard, but this mine is closing. It appears that the best-quality coal has already been used up, and the owners of the mine don't want to use the poor quality coal that remains."

I ask her what she and her husband will do.

"Oh, we won't go hungry! A good miner can always find work. The Canadian Pacific Railway still needs coal, and they've decided to move the mining operation to Banff, where there are fresh, good quality coal mines."

I ask her where Banff is. Will the railway build a whole new town?

She laughs. Banff is only six and a half miles down the road. Believe it or not, the company says they're going to actually move all the houses and buildings to Banff.

"Move all the houses and buildings?" I echo in wonderment.

"We won't be the first town to move. Another town in Alberta, called Wainwright, moved, lock, stock, and barrel."

"So how do the others—your neighbors—feel about all of this?"

"Well, ma'am, I think most of us are going to move, house and all, to Banff, because the company promises jobs to the men. It is beautiful country, and it's lots healthier than living in the city. They say they're going to start moving the buildings next week. I guess the children will have fun watching how they do it!"

She adds, "I'd be glad for you to stay if you want to watch it. Or, give me an address and I'll write and tell you how it goes."

I can't give her an address in the future, so I decide to change my plans and stay for the big move.

Cascade
Mountain
1903

The great day comes and, by the time I get out of bed, the children are lined up on the street, gaping at the buildings that have been placed on huge rollers. Workers are hitching the horses to the rollers. When the horses, straining to pull the rollers, take their first steps, a cheer goes up. The town is on its way! The children dance and jump behind the little parade, shouting, "We're on the move!"

By nightfall, several of the houses, including the Orners', have already been settled in Banff. And so it happens that my last night with the Orner family is spent in an old house in a new town!

POWER SKILL:
Map Reading

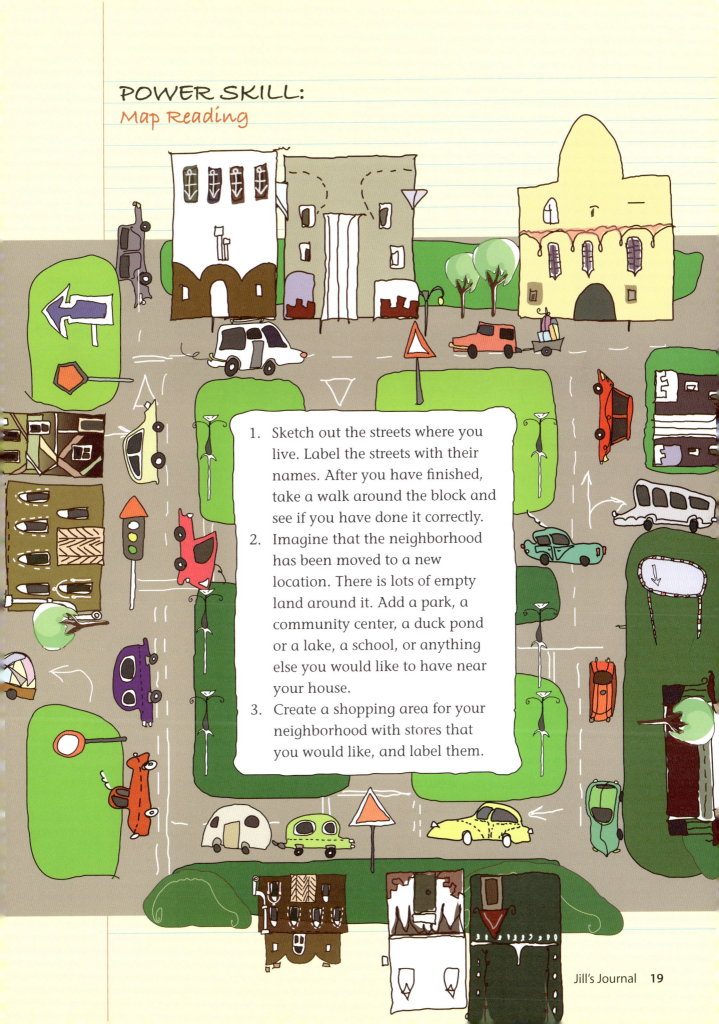

1. Sketch out the streets where you live. Label the streets with their names. After you have finished, take a walk around the block and see if you have done it correctly.

2. Imagine that the neighborhood has been moved to a new location. There is lots of empty land around it. Add a park, a community center, a duck pond or a lake, a school, or anything else you would like to have near your house.

3. Create a shopping area for your neighborhood with stores that you would like, and label them.

Lesson in Literature ...
THE SHORE

WHAT ARE IMAGES?

- An **image** is created by a word or phrase that describes something you can see, hear, smell, taste, or touch.

- A red apple (see), a crunchy apple (hear), a fragrant apple (smell), a sweet apple (taste), and a smooth apple (touch) are all images.

- For visual images, we must *picture* what is being described.

- For other sensory images, we must *remember* and *imagine* the sound, smell, taste, or feel of what is being described.

THINK ABOUT IT!

1. In the description of the sea and the shore, what two images are white?

2. In the description of Cape Cod, which sense would you use to feel each of the following:
   a. the breezes
   b. the ocean spray
   c. the waves

3. a. What sound do the seagulls make?
   b. What color is the bay sky?
   c. What smell comes from the Portuguese bakery?

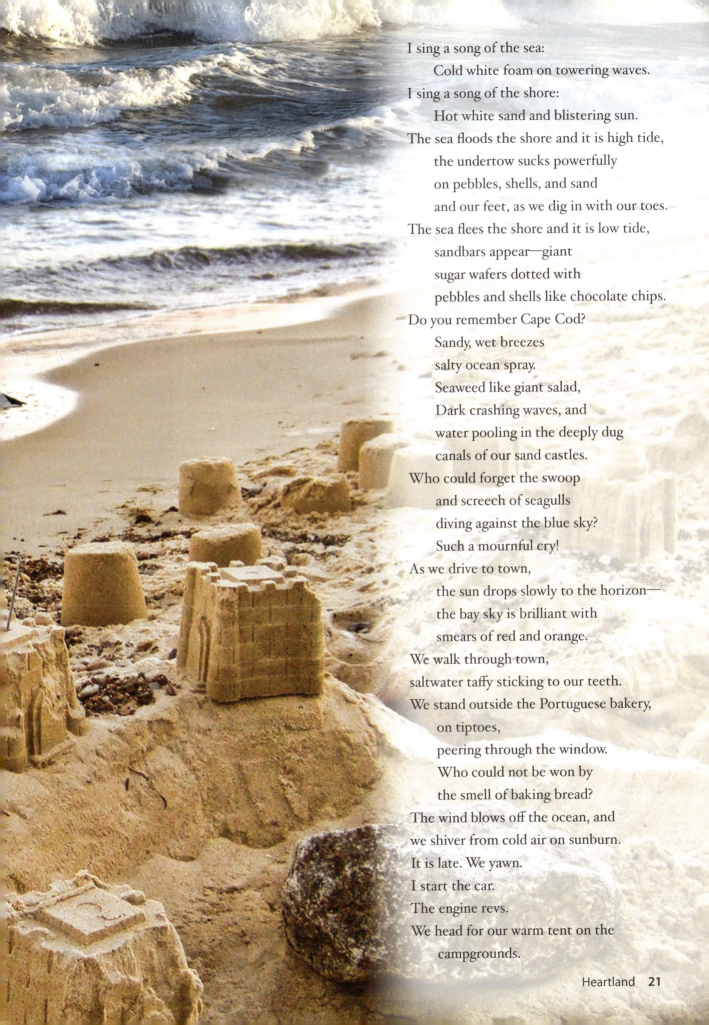

I sing a song of the sea:
    Cold white foam on towering waves.
I sing a song of the shore:
    Hot white sand and blistering sun.
The sea floods the shore and it is high tide,
    the undertow sucks powerfully
    on pebbles, shells, and sand
    and our feet, as we dig in with our toes.
The sea flees the shore and it is low tide,
    sandbars appear—giant
    sugar wafers dotted with
    pebbles and shells like chocolate chips.
Do you remember Cape Cod?
    Sandy, wet breezes
    salty ocean spray.
    Seaweed like giant salad,
    Dark crashing waves, and
    water pooling in the deeply dug
    canals of our sand castles.
Who could forget the swoop
    and screech of seagulls
    diving against the blue sky?
    Such a mournful cry!
As we drive to town,
    the sun drops slowly to the horizon—
    the bay sky is brilliant with
    smears of red and orange.
We walk through town,
saltwater taffy sticking to our teeth.
We stand outside the Portuguese bakery,
    on tiptoes,
    peering through the window.
    Who could not be won by
    the smell of baking bread?
The wind blows off the ocean, and
we shiver from cold air on sunburn.
It is late. We yawn.
I start the car.
The engine revs.
We head for our warm tent on the
    campgrounds.

Blueprint for Reading

INTO . . . *Heartland*

America is beautiful! The country has been blessed with snow-capped mountains and sandy deserts, with lush fields, and deep canyons. Songs and poems have been written about many cities and every state in the U.S.A. Do you know any?

Heartland is a poem about America's Midwest, where so much of our grain and corn are grown. The poet loves the heartland for its beauty, for its changing seasons, and for its fields that supply the entire country with food. As you read *Heartland*, perhaps you will look at where you live with the same loving appreciation that the poet has for America's Heartland.

EYES ON *Images*

Imagine walking outside on a perfect summer day. The sky is blue, the birds are singing, the sun is warm, the clover has a delicious fragrance, and, when you pick a peach off of the tree, it is sweet and juicy. If you wanted to describe this perfect moment to your friend, you would have to use words to describe what you saw, heard, felt, smelled, and tasted. The words you would use create **images**.

Writers like to get their readers to see, hear, feel, smell, and taste things in their imaginations. The poet who wrote *Heartland* wanted her readers to know just how beautiful the farms of the American Midwest are at different times of the year. As you read the poem, you will pass from one image to the next. Try hard to picture the beautiful scenes in your mind.

Heartland

By Diane Siebert

Paintings by Wendell Minor

I am the Heartland,
Great and wide.
I sing of hope.
I sing of pride.

I am the land where wheat fields grow
In golden waves that ebb and flow;
Where cornfields stretched across the plains
Lie green between the country lanes.

I am the Heartland,
Shaped and lined
By rivers, great and small, that wind
Past farms, whose barns and silos stand
Like treasures in my fertile hand.

I am the Heartland.
I can feel
Machines of iron, tools of steel,
Creating farmlands, square by square—
A quilt of life I proudly wear:

WORD BANK

fertile (FUR tuhl) *adj.*: the type of soil or land in which plants grow easily

A patchwork quilt laid gently down
In hues of yellow, green, and brown
As tractors, plows, and planters go
Across my fields and, row by row,
Prepare the earth and plant the seeds
That grow to meet a nation's needs.

A patchwork quilt whose seams are etched
By miles of wood and wire stretched
Around the barns and pastures where
The smell of livestock fills the air.
These are the farms where hogs are bred,
The farms where chicks are hatched and fed;
The farms where dairy cows are raised,
The farms where cattle herds are grazed;
The farms with horses, farms with sheep—
Upon myself, all these I keep.

I am the Heartland.
On this soil
Live those who through the seasons toil:

The farmer, with his spirit strong;
The farmer, working hard and long,
A feed-and-seed-store cap in place,
Pulled down to shield a weathered face—
A face whose every crease and line
Can tell a tale, and help define
A lifetime spent beneath the sun,
A life of work that's never done.

I am the Heartland.
On these plains
Rise elevators filled with grains.
They mark the towns where people walk
To see their neighbors, just to talk;
Where farmers go to get supplies
And sit a spell to analyze
The going price of corn and beans,
The rising cost of new machines;
Where steps are meant for shelling peas,
And kids build houses in the trees.

WORD BANK

toil (TOYL) *n.*: hard work

weathered (WEH thurd) *adj.*: roughened by the weather

define (dee FINE) *v.*: explain

I am the Heartland.
In my song
Are cities beating, steady, strong,
With footsteps from a million feet
And sounds of traffic in the street;
Where giant mills and stockyards sprawl,
And neon-lighted shadows fall
From windowed walls of brick that rise
Toward the clouds, to scrape the skies;
Where highways meet and rails converge;
Where farm and city rhythms merge
To form a vital bond between
The concrete and the fields of green.

I am the Heartland:
Earth and sky
And changing seasons passing by.

I feel the touch of autumn's chill,
And as its colors brightly spill
Across the land, the growing ends,

And winter, white and cold, descends
With blizzards howling as they sweep
Across me, piling snowdrifts deep.
Then days grow longer, skies turn clear,
And all the gifts of spring appear—
The young are born, the seedlings sprout;

WORD BANK
stockyards (STOCK yards) *n.*: a yard for livestock
converge (kuhn VURJ) *v.*: meet
merge (MURJ) *v.*: come together
vital (VIE tul) *adj.*: extremely important
descends (dih SENDS) *v.*: comes down

Before me, summer stretches out
With pastures draped in lush, green grass,
And as the days of growing pass,
I feel the joy when fields of grain
Are blessed by sunlight, warmth, and rain;

For I have learned of drought and hail,
Of floods and frosts and crops that fail,
And of tornadoes as they move
In frightening paths, again to prove
That in the Heartland, on these plains,
Despite Man's power, Nature reigns.

WORD BANK

drought (DROWT) *n.*:
a lack of rain

I am the Heartland.
Smell the fields,
The rich, dark earth, and all it yields;
The air before a coming storm,
A newborn calf, so damp and warm;
The dusty grain in barns that hold
The bales of hay, all green and gold.

I am the Heartland.
Hear me speak
In voices raised by those who seek
To live their lives upon the land,
To know and love and understand
The secrets of a living earth—
Its strengths, its weaknesses, its worth;
Who, Heartland born and Heartland bred,
Possess the will to move ahead.

I am the Heartland.
I survive
To keep America, my home, alive.

ABOUT THE AUTHOR

In the 1970s, **Diane Siebert** decided to take a summer trip with her husband. They left their jobs, sold some of their belongings, bought two motorcycles, and began traveling throughout the United States. The trip lasted ten years! Every night, Ms. Siebert wrote in her journal about her experiences of that day, and she later transformed the material in her journal into poetry and children's books celebrating the beauty of America. Today, Ms. Siebert lives in Crooked River Ranch, Oregon.

ABOUT THE ILLUSTRATOR

Wendell Minor knew by fourth grade that he wanted to be an artist. He began by doodling on the edges of his test papers. Today, Mr. Minor has won hundreds of awards for his art and illustrations, and he has even designed stamps for the U.S. Postal Service. Mr. Minor always visits the places he paints in order to see them firsthand. Because of this research he has traveled throughout the U.S. In his art, Mr. Minor combines his loves of nature and American history. Through his illustrations, Mr. Minor hopes to inspire children to appreciate the beauty in nature.

Studying the Selection

America is beautiful from sea to shining sea, but everyone has their own favorite part of the United States. Which region do you think is the most beautiful?

QUICK REVIEW

1. Who (or what) is the narrator of the poem?

2. Explain how farmland can look like a patchwork quilt.

3. What are three sights one could see in a city that are described in the poem?

4. The Heartland says that it keeps America alive. How does the Heartland keep America alive?

FOCUS

5. The poem says that the people in the Heartland seek

   "To know and love and understand
   The secrets of a living earth"

   What secrets does the earth have? One secret might be how to make the corn grow big and tall. Can you think of another secret the farmers would like to learn?

6. The poet wanted the reader to imagine how the fields and livestock look and feel and even smell. Below are four lines taken from the poem. Which ones help you imagine how things look? Which ones help you imagine how things feel?

   "In golden waves that ebb and flow"
   "I feel the touch of autumn's chill"
   "Where cornfields stretched across the plains"
   "A newborn calf, so damp and warm"

CREATING AND WRITING

7. Choose one area that you know well. You may choose your block, your town, a park that you visit, or any other familiar spot. Write a 4–6 line poem about it. (The lines do not have to rhyme.) Use at least three images in your poem.

8. Your teacher will distribute the materials necessary to create a display with three sections. Choose three images from the poem and draw a picture of each one of them for each part of your display. You can paste objects on your drawings.

Lesson in Literature ...

DESCRIPTIVE TEXT

- A good author will provide *details* that bring the reader into the time and place of the story. For example, if the story speaks of horses and buggies, the reader knows without being told that the story takes place before cars were invented.

- *Mood* is part of setting. Mood is the feeling the story creates. Is the story happy? Scary? Sad? All those are moods.

- *Sound* can be part of setting. If the story talks of birds singing or thunder crashing, the sound contributes to the setting.

- *Light* can be part of setting. Does the story take place under the bright sun? In a dark cave? In a gloomy basement? All these are part of setting.

THINK ABOUT IT!

1. What are two details that tell you when the story takes place?

2. What is the mood of the story?

3. Imagine that you are with the two boys sitting on the hilltop, playing a game of *I Spy*. One of you spies something blue. One of you spies something green. One of you spies something white. What is it that each one of you is "spying"?

Tom and Tola played together most days. Tom's real name was Thomas and Tola's real name was Amitola, which is Sioux for "rainbow." Tom lived on one side of the hill with his family, pioneers who had come to South Dakota the year before. They had staked out some land, planted some crops, and built a barn for their livestock. Amitola lived on the other side of the hill. His family were Sioux Indians. They grew some crops, fished, and hunted buffalo. The people from both sides of the hill got along peacefully, but couldn't communicate very well, because the Sioux spoke Sioux language and the pioneers spoke English.

It was morning and, as usual, Tom and Amitola met each other right at the top of the hill. Tola knew a bit of English and Tom knew a bit of Sioux. When they got stuck, they drew pictures to let each other know what they meant.

"We got an armchair today," said Tom to Tola. "It was sent all the way from Boston. My, oh my, but it's grand! My pa looks like a king when he sits on it."

"An armchair?" said Tola. "You put your arms in a chair? Where do you put your feet?"

TOM AND TOLA TALK

"No, no, no!" said Tom. "It's not a chair *for* your arms, it's a chair *with* arms."

"A chair of arms?" said Tola, amazed. He pictured a kind of octopus that one sits in.

"No, no, no! The sides of the chair have a place for your arms to rest."

"Your arms are tired?" asked Tola.

"Listen," said Tom with exasperation. "Come to my house at two o'clock and you'll see it."

"What time is two o'clock?" asked Tola.

"You know," said Tom. "It's when the hands of the clock point at the twelve and the two."

"The clock has real hands?" asked Tola, imagining a clock wearing gloves in the cold weather.

"No, no, no! On the clock's face, there are two long pieces of metal that move."

"The clock has the face of a man?" exclaimed Tola, imagining a smiling clock wearing a hat to go with its gloves.

"No, no, no!" said Tom. "The front of the clock is called the face, and the metal pointers are called the hands. When the hands move to a certain time, the clock rings."

"Rings?" wondered Tola. "The hands wear rings?"

"No, no, no!" said Tom. "Here, I'd better draw a picture for you."

Tom drew a picture of a clock with two

hands and a bell for an alarm. He showed Tola how it worked.

Then Tola pointed to the sky. "You see the sun up there?"

"Sure," said Tom.

"Do you see how it has moved since we first got up here on the hill?"

"Yes," said Tom.

"Look up. What do you see?"

"I see a beautiful blue sky with two white clouds in it."

"Well, when the sun reaches the middle of the sky, it will be twelve o'clock."

Tom nodded.

"Now, look over there," said Tola. "What do you see?"

"I see some green trees at the top of another hill. I see some deer on the hill and some wildflowers in the grass."

"Well," said Tola, "when the sun reaches the top of those trees, it will be two o'clock. You see, I do not need any clocks wearing rings on their hands with funny faces. I just need the shining sun and the beautiful sky. And, when the sun reaches the treetops, I will come to your house and see the chair that has arms. By the way, does it also have legs?" asked Tola slyly.

"Of course!" answered Tom, as he turned to run down the grassy hill.

Blueprint for Reading

INTO . . . *No Laughing Matter*

Memories of good times are like jigsaw puzzles. They include a little piece of this and a bigger piece of that. All the little pieces fit together to form a beautiful picture. What do you remember about a day at an amusement park? The bright sun? The loud music? The tantalizing smell of roasted peanuts? Perhaps your strongest memory is the sense of victory you felt when you climbed off of the highest, fastest roller coaster you'd ever tried. For almost everyone, spending time with family or friends in a relaxed atmosphere is a very important piece of their memory "puzzle." As you read *No Laughing Matter*, picture yourself as one of the kids who go to the amusement park, and count how many puzzle pieces are at work creating this beautiful picture.

EYES ON *Descriptive Text*

When you think of a story that you have read, most of the time it is the plot or the characters that come to mind. Sometimes, though, what you remember about a story is its setting. If you actually went to where the story took place, you would feel that you'd been there before. There are two settings in *No Laughing Matter*. One is the children's backyard in "anywhere USA." The city is not named (though it must be near Euclid Beach Park), but it is clearly an ordinary town where houses have backyards and the neighbors are friendly. The second setting was once a real place: Euclid Beach Park, an amusement park in Cleveland, Ohio. The story brings to mind the sounds, smells, and excitement that every amusement park provides. In the background of both settings is something we all remember: the slow days of summer, when school is out and kids can let their imaginations run free.

No Laughing Matter

Abigail Rozen

It was hot, almost too hot to play ball. The three of us sat on the front lawn lazily plucking blades of grass and looking for puffy old dandelions to blow at each other. The bat and ball lay on the grass, waiting for us to pick them up.

"Let's play Batter Up," I said.

"It's too hot," said my cousin Earl. Earl was spending part of the summer with us. He lived in New York City where, according to him, it was hot enough to fry an egg on the sidewalk. I didn't believe him, but since he was our guest, and two years older than me, I let it go.

"Dad says it's never too hot to play baseball," said Pete, my kid brother.

Dad believed in baseball like a dentist believes in brushing teeth. Dad had taught each of us how to hold a bat when we were only three years old. "Choke up,"[1] he would yell as I struggled to hold a bat that was bigger than I was. "Baseball is no laughing matter."

But his work had paid off, and I was the best baseball player of all the girls in my third grade class.

---

1. *Choke up* is a phrase used to describe the proper way to hold a bat. The hands should be near the bottom of the bat and one hand should be right above the other. There should be no space between one hand and the other.

"Let's not start a game now. We'll be leaving in a few minutes," said Earl.

We all perked up when we heard that. Every Sunday in the summer, our parents took us on a trip. We'd been to the zoo, the aquarium, and lots of state parks. But today we were going to our favorite place in the world, Euclid Beach Park. Euclid Beach was an amusement park right next to Lake Erie, and the rides were awesome.

Mom and Dad came outside and off we went in our shiny new Chevy. A half an hour later we pulled into the crowded parking lot. Almost jumping out of the car, we headed for the entrance. As we approached the iron gates, the smell of popcorn wafted toward us. A moment later, the sound of carousel music greeted us.

My father bought the admission tickets and we were in. But, as usual, we didn't get too far. That's because Laughing Sal was right next to the ticket booth. Laughing Sal was a huge dummy who looked like a lady with very red cheeks and a great big smile, wearing a housedress with a white apron over it. She swayed back and forth and laughed and laughed and laughed. No one could pass her without laughing.

Most people watched Laughing Sal for a few minutes and then headed for the rides. But not Pete. Pete could never tear himself away from Laughing Sal. He would stand watching her, swaying along with her and laughing his head off. Dad usually had to pick him up and carry him to the ride that was going to be our first stop. Today was no different.

As the sound of Laughing Sal faded behind us, we joined the line to get onto the Bug, Earl's favorite ride. All of us climbed into a car shaped like a ladybug, and held on for dear life as the Bug sprang alive and sped up, down, and around a track, blowing hats off and making us shriek with fear and fun.

WORD BANK
wafted (WAHF ted) *v*.: floated through the air
carousel (KER uh SEL) *n*.: a merry-go-round

"I am so dizzy," laughed Pete as we climbed out of the Bug.

"Where to next?" Dad said, looking at Mom.

"How about that new ride called the Rotor? I've heard a lot about it," said Mom. Mom loved anything that was new and unusual. I wished I was more like that.

In the distance, we saw some flashing lights that spelled out *Rotor*, and we made a beeline for it. We walked out of the bright sunlight into a building that consisted of a big, round room whose walls were made of rubber!

"I feel like I'm standing inside a tire," whispered Earl.

We all took our places around the circumference of the room.

"Lean back against the walls," said the announcer.

Slowly, the room started to go around and around.

"The floor's sinking!" yelled Earl.

As the room whirled faster and faster, the floor sank lower and lower! But we didn't go with it. We were stuck to the rubber walls with no floor to stand on! Looking across the room, each of us saw everyone attached to the wall, feet dangling in the air, far above the floor. We all began to laugh.

Then the spinning walls slowed down.

"Loosen your backs and slide down slowly," came the announcement.

> ## WORD BANK
>
> **circumference** (sur KUM fer unts) *n.*: the border of a circle

The riders did that, landing softly on the floor. The room slowly came to a halt, and we all filed out, speculating about why we'd stayed stuck to the walls when the floor dropped.

"Now it's your turn to choose a ride, Caroline," said my Dad.

Although I'd tried to hide it, the Bug terrified me, and, when I was in the Rotor, I was afraid I would stay stuck to the rubber walls forever. So I chose a nice, safe, un-scary ride.

"I'd like to go on—"

"The Kentucky Derby," said Earl and Pete in unison. They knew me all too well!

The Kentucky Derby was like a merry-go-round but a little more exciting. The horses on it looked like race horses and the carousel went around very fast. Pete and I knew all the different horses on it.

WORD BANK

speculating (SPEK yoo LAYT ing) *v.*: giving possible reasons for something

"Race you to the black stallion," yelled Pete, running ahead. But I was faster than he was and got there first. I leaped onto the black horse and Pete had to be content with the white one next to mine.

After lots more rides, a picnic supper, and huge tufts of cotton candy, we headed for home, tired but happy. It had been a great day. I was just nodding off in the car when Pete began to shriek.

"What is it?" asked Mom worriedly, turning around to the back seat. Pete just continued to shriek.

"Pete! What's wrong?" asked Dad, without turning around because he was driving.

Pete pointed at a beetle crawling up the leg of his pants.

"Oh, it's just a beetle," said Earl. "I think I'll save it for my bug collection." He took a paper cup and guided the beetle into it, and put the cup into a paper bag.

"This is the first I'm hearing of a bug collection," said Mom nervously.

"Don't worry, Aunt Katie," said Earl. "I keep it in the garage."

Mom sighed, looking relieved.

WORD BANK

tufts *n.*: a bunch of cottony or feathery material

On Monday, the sun shone out of a bright blue sky, but it was a little cooler. We spent the day swimming at the neighborhood pool, having a picnic lunch packed by my mother, and playing Running Bases in our backyard. All day long we replayed our day at Euclid Beach. We debated about which ride was the best, the scariest, the safest, or the most fun. We even tried to invent new rides. After supper, Earl and I went back outside to the backyard. Our neighbor, Mrs. Williams, was enjoying the evening air with her dog, Brownie.

"Hi, kids," said Mrs. Williams.

We walked across to Mrs. Williams' yard and petted Brownie, who, as Dad said, was the tail-wagging-est dog he'd ever seen. We were glad Mrs. Williams had such a friendly dog, because she always looked a little sad. Mom had told us that her husband had died a short while before she'd moved next door, so we should be especially nice to her. The telephone rang inside, and Mrs. Williams jumped up to get it. Brownie stayed outside, delighted to have some friends.

> ## WORD BANK
>
> **debated** (dih BAYT ed)
> *v*.: argued

We heard someone laughing in our backyard and we turned around to see who it was. Standing on a kitchen stool, wearing a big white apron and a lot of red face paint on his cheeks, was Pete, laughing and swaying. On his head was the wig Mom wore when she dressed up like a clown for her kindergarteners.

We ran over to him and couldn't help laughing along. Brownie, though, wasn't amused. He began to howl! A few seconds later, we heard some screaming and yowling coming from the yard on the other side of our house. It was Mrs. Fenster's two tiger cats, who'd come outside and were almost shrieking!

"What's all that racket?" called my father from inside the house.

"Oh, it's nothing," I called back, motioning to Pete to stop laughing.

He did, and the racket stopped.

"What were you doing?" I said, though I thought I knew.

"Didn't you recognize me?" said Pete. "I was Laughing Sal!"

"You were pretty good!" said Earl.

"Earl's right," I said. "I couldn't help laughing along, just the way I do when I pass Laughing Sal. But you'd better put all that stuff away and wash off the red. Dad is not happy about your working up the dogs and cats in the neighborhood."

"Okay," said Pete. "But let's do this again a different time."

He ran back into the house and came back out in his own clothes with his face scrubbed.

Tuesday was not much different from Monday. In fact, it was almost exactly the same. Swimming in the morning, picnic lunch, throwing a baseball around in the afternoon. I was bored.

"I bet I can hit a ball farther than you can," I said to Earl.

Earl didn't answer. He just began to laugh. First he laughed softly, then he laughed louder and louder until he was doubled over. Finally, he choked out one word.

"*You*?" he said.

I was beginning to get mad.

"Yeah, me," I said.

Getting control of himself, Earl said, "Okay, let's have a contest. One of us will pitch to the other and we'll mark how far the ball went. Then we'll reverse it. Do you want to

bat first or pitch first?"

"I'll pitch first," I said.

Earl looked at our small backyard.

"We'd better do this in the driveway. That will give me plenty of distance. If we do it in the backyard, the ball will go way out the back and into those trees behind your yard."

"Okay," I said. A little voice in the back of my mind told me that our driveway was very close to Mrs. Williams' house. But her windows were really high up, I reasoned, and nothing would happen to them.

Earl picked up the bat and walked all the way to the end of our driveway, almost into the street, but not quite. I pitched. Swing

and a miss. I pitched again. Earl jumped back and yelled "low and inside." Personally, I thought he was just being dramatic, but I wound up for the next pitch.

SMACK! The ball went straight up our driveway, headed for the garage, and hit the top of the garage, just missing the windows on the garage door.

"We can't really know how far that ball would have gone if it hadn't been stopped by the garage," said Earl. "But it's okay. You can take your turn now."

I could see the smug look on Earl's face. He was sure I couldn't even get the ball as far as the garage, so he wasn't worried about proving that his would have gone farther.

I went to where he'd laid "home plate" and got ready.

"Ball one!" yelled Pete, as he ran across the street to get the ball.

"Did you look both ways before you ran?" I yelled at him.

"Yeah," he yelled back, tossing the ball back to Earl.

Earl wound up and sent one straight over the plate. I hit it with everything I had. We all watched the ball as it soared high over the driveway, higher than any of us could have imagined, high enough to—CRASH! High enough to break one of Mrs. Williams' windows!

The three of us ran over to the pile of glass that had fallen on our driveway. We were speechless. Out came Mrs. Williams.

"What happened? I heard a crash on my second floor! Do you think one of those pigeons banged into my window?"

"No," said Earl. "It wasn't a pigeon."

Mrs. Williams looked at the three of us, looked at the mitt, and looked at the bat.

"Oh," she said.

At that moment, Mom came outside.

"What's going on?" she said.

Before we could answer, she took in the situation.

"Who is responsible for this?" she asked sternly.

"I hit the ball," I heard myself saying in a tiny voice.

"Were all three of you playing?" asked Mom insistently.

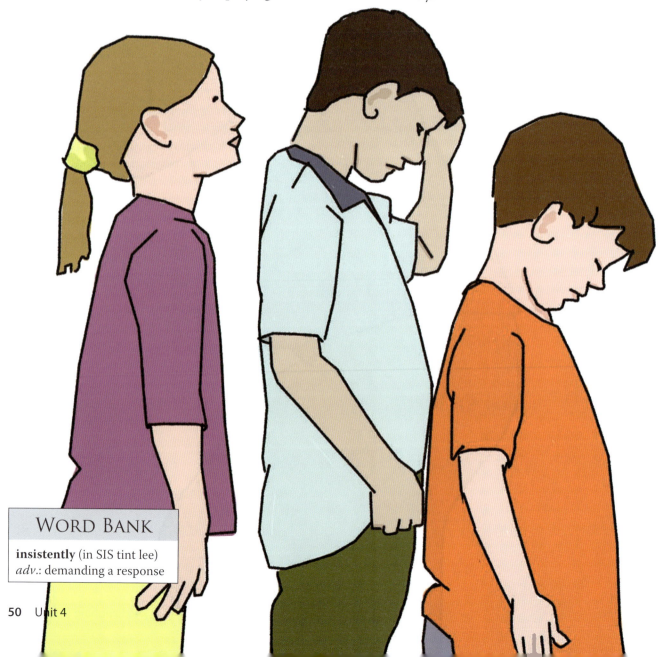

> ### WORD BANK
>
> **insistently** (in SIS tint lee)
> *adv.*: demanding a response

"Yes," said Earl.

"Don't you remember my telling you not to play ball in the driveway?" asked Mom. We all nodded.

"I'm sorry," I said.

"Being sorry is a good first step. But what are we going to do about Mrs. Williams' broken window?" asked Mom.

"Pay for it?" said Earl.

"We will have to pay for it," said Mom. "How do you suggest we do that?"

"I have thirteen cents," said Pete.

"And I have three dollars left from my birthday," I said.

"My mother gave me five dollars of spending money and I have three of it left," said Earl.

"It will cost about ten dollars to fix Mrs. Williams' window. I don't think we should use any of Pete's money, but we can use one dollar of Caroline's and one dollar of Earl's. That will give us two dollars. I will pay five dollars toward the window, and you children will have to earn another three. Next time, I hope you will be careful not to hit any balls where they can break a window."

Mom went back inside to get a broom to sweep up the glass.

We looked at each other. How were we going to earn three dollars? We could collect empty pop bottles and cash them in, but we would only get two cents a bottle. It would take forever to raise three dollars.

"Why don't we make an amusement park?" said Pete.

"Sure," I said glumly. "I'll build a roller coaster."

"We could get at least ten kids to come, and if we charge them each ten cents that would be …" He paused. Arithmetic was not his strongest subject.

"One dollar," said Earl.

"We could ask Aunt Katie to make popcorn and sell it for a dime a bag," said Earl. "If we sold ten bags, that would be another dollar."

"What about the last dollar?" I asked.

"We'll work on that tomorrow," said Earl.

"What are we going to use for the rides?" I asked.

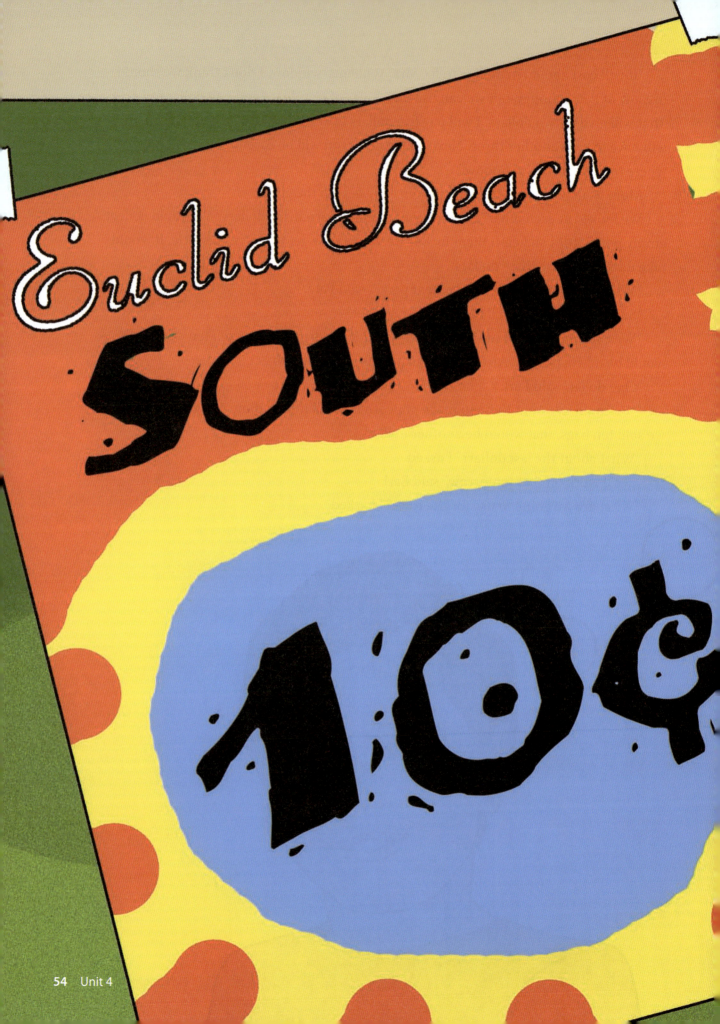

"Here's my idea," said Pete.

At 6:30 the next evening there was a line down our driveway. At the top of the driveway, Earl stood behind a folding table selling tickets. Taped to the table was a poster saying *Euclid Beach South.* Everyone in line could smell the hot, buttered popcorn being sold at the table next to the "ticket booth." On a little stand nearby, a record player was playing loud circus music. Almost every child, after paying ten cents for admission, headed straight to the popcorn booth and bought a bag of popcorn for ten cents.

Earl, Pete, and I had spent all afternoon setting up the booths and making the signs for them. There were six altogether.

Each ticket holder could visit all six booths. As the children made their way through the booths, the others waited their turn, laughing and chattering. The sign over our shed read, *See the Dangerous African Tigers!* In front of a tree that we'd surrounded with sheets was a poster that said *Ride the Rotor.* In front of a refrigerator crate was a sign that said *The Euclid Beach Bug.* *The Kentucky Derby* was located in one half of our garage, and *The Flesh-Eating Cannibal* was in the other half. A *Yukon Wolf Habitat* was in the crawl space beneath our back steps.

At first, the children were happy and laughing. But after a short while, they started to grumble. After several of the children had gone through the booths, they gathered into a tight little circle, their voices growing louder and louder. Finally, they turned to Earl and yelled, "We want our money back!" Earl looked uncomfortable. "Why?" he asked.

"You call this an amusement park?" yelled one of them.

I began to worry. Where was Pete? This was all his idea. He should have been here to explain. Anyway, he'd promised he was going to surprise us with a really good booth.

More and more of the kids were joining the protest.

"These are supposed to be 'dangerous African tigers'?" yelled Mike who lived down the block. "They're just Mrs. Fenster's cats!"

"And 'the Bug'? You *know* we thought it would be like the ride, not a real bug!"

"It really did come from Euclid Beach," said Earl defensively. "Pete brought it back on his pants leg."

"Some Yukon Wolf!" growled Anthony.

"Mrs. Williams says he has some wolf blood in him."

"Brownie? You know he's nothin' but a mutt."

Brownie, upon hearing his name, came out of the crawl space and began to wag his tail.

"But didn't you like the Rotor?" I asked.

"Are you kidding?" said Nate. "You call being pushed around in a rubber tire a Rotor ride?"

"And the flesh-eating cannibals," hollered Rosie. "They're nothing more than some guppies."

"Well, they do eat each other," I said meekly.

"Yeah, but we don't need to pay a dime to see some fish, or to sit on your kid brother's rocking horse and call it the Kentucky Derby."

They all surrounded Earl and started to chant: "We want our money back! Give us our money back!"

All of a sudden, over the chanting, I heard someone laugh. It wasn't a normal laugh. It was laughing and laughing and laughing—it was Laughing Sal!

I ran over to Pete who was all dressed up in Mom's clown wig, Dad's white barbecuing apron, and painted red cheeks, standing and swaying on the kitchen stool.

"Where have you been all this time?" I whispered fiercely.

"I couldn't find the wig. But now I'm ready."

Louder and louder Pete laughed. One by one the kids turned around and went to gawk at him. And one by one they began to laugh along with him. Our neighbor Mrs. Williams came outside. Walking over to our backyard, she saw Pete. A little smile crossed her face, then it grew … and grew … until she was grinning. Finally, she burst out laughing and laughed until the tears rolled down her face.

> **WORD BANK**
>
> **gawk** (GAWK) *v.*: stare

When everyone finally quieted down, and even Pete couldn't laugh anymore, the children quietly left the yard with a smile and a thank you. Nobody asked for their money back.

When everyone had left, Mrs. Williams turned to Pete and said, "Peter, I haven't laughed like that since my husband passed away. I can't thank you enough for helping me to feel happy again."

She looked around and noticed the ticket booth.

"You know, I didn't pay for my admission. Let me do that now." She took a dollar out of her pocket and added it to the two dollars that were in the cigar box.

"I'm paying a dollar, but really, what you've given me, Peter, is priceless."

With that, she gave Pete a little hug and said, "Come Brownie, let's go home."

ABOUT THE AUTHOR

Abigail Rozen loves to read and write children's stories. In fact, one of her all-time favorite stories is right in this book: *A Toad for Tuesday*. Mrs. Rozen was born in Cleveland, Ohio. As a child, Mrs. Rozen and her family drove in their shiny new Chevy to Euclid Beach Park, where they rode the Bug, clung to the walls of the Rotor, and sped around on the Kentucky Derby. One thing Mrs. Rozen has never done is ride a roller coaster. "My life is thrilling enough as it is," she says. "If I want some ups and downs, I ride an elevator."

Studying the Selection

What do you do during the long summer days? Do you like scheduled activities or would you rather just plan each day as it comes?

QUICK REVIEW

1. What sport was very important to Dad and the kids?

2. What was Pete's favorite part of Euclid Beach Park?

3. Why was Mrs. Williams sad?

4. How did the children hope to raise two of the three dollars they needed?

FOCUS

5. What were at least four things that helped the children enjoy their day at Euclid Beach Park?

6. Mood is an important part of setting. The mood changes in different parts of the story. Describe the mood

   a. at the opening of the story.

   b. as the children walked into Euclid Beach Park.

   c. when the neighborhood kids started to demand their money back.

   d. when Pete starts to laugh and laugh at the end of the story.

CREATING AND WRITING

7. Every setting has its own sights, sounds, and smells. Choose one of the following and write a paragraph describing what a person would be seeing, hearing, and smelling when he entered that place:

   a. The beach

   b. An airport

   c. The zoo

8. On the day after they visited Euclid Beach Park, the children discussed the rides and even "tried to invent new rides." Draw a picture of a ride you have invented. Make sure you give your ride a name and include a sign with the name of the ride in your picture. Under the picture, write a brief description of the ride and any instructions for the rider.

Lesson in Literature...
SARAH AND THE
SAN FRANCISCO EARTHQUAKE

HISTORICAL FICTION

- **Historical fiction** is partly true and partly made up.

- Usually, the setting is described as it really was, and some or all of the characters are made up.

- The writer makes up characters to help the reader feel what it was like to be living at a certain time.

- For historical fiction to be good, the author must do a lot of research about the time period that is being described.

The conversation, clothing, and behavior of the characters must all sound *authentic*—they must be true to life.

THINK ABOUT IT!

1. What was the date of the famous San Francisco Earthquake?

2. Why did the children have to leave their house?

3. Where did the people whose houses had burned down stay for a while?

A grandmother sat in a rocking chair with her cat on her lap. Her six grandchildren were sitting in a circle at her feet on an oval braided rug, sipping mugs of hot chocolate. There was a fire burning in the fireplace. The wood crackled and sparked. "Grandma! Grandma!" they cried. "Tell us a story about San Francisco!"

They liked to hear stories from long ago about their hometown. She thought for a moment. "How about a story about a girl named Sarah? She lived a long time ago when my grandma was alive." They all nodded yes.

She continued, "Sarah was a very brave young girl. This is her story."

Sarah and her family lived happily in a small house in San Francisco. Very early in the morning on Wednesday, April 18, 1906, she was awakened from her sleep by a jolt. It was as though the ground under the bed was falling away. Sarah was sleeping with her two little sisters. Both of them awoke and tried to hold on to her. Then the shaking stopped. They had had minor earthquakes before.

Then the stronger, more frightening shaking began. Sarah's sisters were crying. Her mother and father were already at work. Her mother was a housekeeper and started working at 4:30 a.m. Her father was a firefighter. He had slept at the firehouse.

Sarah ordered her sisters to lie flat on their stomachs on the bed. She tried to speak calmly. She covered their heads with pillows. Then she lay on top of them and held a pillow over her head. They did this very quickly.

It seemed as though the shaking would never stop. It lasted about a minute, but it seemed like a much longer time to Sarah. It felt like the ground was falling away and she worried that the house might collapse.

Sarah knew from her father that when an earthquake comes, if you are in bed you stay in bed, as long as the bed is not near windows or the outside wall.

The shaking stopped. The children waited to see if there was going to be another big shock. When it did not come, Sarah said, "We must get dressed very quickly!" She stuffed clothing for her family in a basket. Then she gathered together food in a burlap sack: all the bread, cheese, and dried apples the family had. She took a bottle that was filled with water. She was afraid this would be too heavy, but knew they needed some food. Sarah then thought they better leave the house and try to find their parents.

As they stepped outdoors, they could smell smoke and burning. Father had once said that it would be possible during an earthquake for gas mains to break. Then the gas could catch fire. But, he said, that hadn't happened yet. Now it seemed to have happened. What would happen to their house?

The children walked together in the middle of the road. It was a long walk to where their mother worked. By the time they got there, Sarah could see that parts of the city were on fire. Would her father be all right?

Their mother was still there—although the house she was working in was badly damaged. She ran to them and cried out, "Sarah, I knew I could trust you to come with the girls. I worried that if I set out looking for you, we might not find each other very easily." Mother lifted the burlap bag from Sarah's arms. Inside it she put little cakes and more bread that she had gotten from the people she worked for. Sarah took the clothing basket from her little sisters.

They all headed for the firehouse where they found Father. They later learned that their house had burned to the ground with 25,000 others. Like so many other San Franciscans, that night they began their life in a tent. As they struggled to put up the tent, Mother said, "We must be grateful we are alive and unharmed, and that your father is safe. We will live bravely and happily in a small tent for as long as necessary."

Blueprint for Reading

INTO . . . *Patrick and the Great Molasses Explosion*

All of us have heard stories about earthquakes or floods or animals escaping from the zoo, but have you ever tried to imagine what it would feel like to actually *be* there? When major events are happening, most people don't even realize that history is being made. They see what is happening right around them, but are not sure what is happening everywhere else. Only later do they find out that they were a part of something important.

When a little red-haired boy named Patrick sees molasses flowing down the street, he knows *something* is happening, but little does he realize how much is happening!

EYES ON *Historical Fiction*

When a story is interesting, the first question we usually ask is, "Is it true?" That question is not always easily answered. Some stories are completely true. Others are completely made up. But some are a blend of the two. You have learned that every story has a plot, a setting, and characters. When all three are true, the story is **nonfiction**. When one or more of those elements is made up, the story is **fiction**. For example, if the setting is real, but the plot and characters are made up, the story is fiction.

Sometimes an author knows of a true story and wants to tell it in an exciting way, so the author tells the true story, but makes up some of the characters. That kind of story is called **historical fiction**. It is *historical*, because the events and setting are true. It is *fiction*, because the characters are made up. As you read *Patrick and the Great Molasses Explosion*, see if you can separate *fact* from *fiction*.

Patrick and the Great Molasses Explosion

Marjorie Stover

There once was a boy named Patrick McGonnigal[1] O'Brien. He had red hair and freckles, and he lived with his mama, his papa, and his two-year-old sister, Mary, in the city of Boston.

Now if there was one thing in this wide world that Patrick had a fondness and a craving for, it was molasses. He had molasses on his oatmeal for breakfast. He had molasses on his pancakes for lunch. For supper he had Boston brown bread and baked beans sweetened with molasses.

1. *McGonnigal* (muh GON ih gul)

Still, Patrick had never had enough molasses to satisfy his craving. He was always trying to get another lick. When Mama filled the molasses pitcher from the tin pail, he was right there to run his finger along the edge and lick up the dribbles.

One day when Mama's back was turned, Patrick stuck his finger into the pitcher to sneak a lick. In his hurry he tipped the pitcher over! Mama turned around just as the molasses poured out in a gooey, brown puddle on the tablecloth.

"Patrick McGonnigal O'Brien! See what you've done!" scolded Mama. The red bun of hair on the back of her head waggled from side to side. She scraped up the molasses with a spoon, but not one drop did Patrick get.

Every Sunday afternoon Papa took Patrick for a walk down along the harbor to see all the wonderful sights. Horses and buggies clattered over the cobblestones. New-fangled[2] automobiles tooted their horns. Overhead, a train clacked along the raised tracks.

In the harbor they saw all kinds of boats—freighters, steamboats, tugboats, and sailboats. Together they stood on a freight-loading platform where Papa worked on weekdays. Patrick liked to brag that Papa could load and unload boxes and barrels as fast as the fastest man there, and maybe a wee bit faster.

---

2. *New-fangled* is an old-fashioned word for modern and complicated.

WORD BANK

clattered (KLATT erd) *v.*: made a loud, rattling sound

cobblestones (KAH bl STONES) *n.*: a naturally rounded stone that was used to pave streets

They always stopped in the stable to see the big Belgian work horses that pulled the heavy freight wagons. Now and then Patrick slipped a sugar lump to one of the horses. Papa teased Patrick that the horses liked sugar as much as Patrick liked molasses.

The most wonderful sight of all, however, was a huge, enormous tank as tall as a four-story building. The tank was made of big sheets of metal fastened together with rivets. Patrick could see the large, round heads of the rivets pounded in neat rows along the seams. Painted in big letters on the round sides of the tank were the words, PURITY DISTILLING COMPANY. This giant tank was filled with molasses. Papa had said so.

The very thought of so much molasses made Patrick's mouth water. Sometimes Patrick dreamed that he was seated on the edge of the tank with a giant straw just sucking, sucking, sucking molasses all day long.

WORD BANK

enormous (ih NORR muss) *adj.*: huge

rivets (RIH vets) *n.*: metal pins that go through two or more pieces of metal, holding them together

One winter day when Patrick arrived home from school for lunch, Mama said, "Eat your soup and crackers, and don't delay. I've a fancy to make oatmeal molasses cookies this afternoon, but the molasses pail is empty. If you hurry, you can get it filled at the corner store before you go back to school."

At the thought of molasses cookies, Patrick's green eyes twinkled. He slurped down his soup as fast as he could. He pulled on his cap, buttoned his jacket, and hooked the wire handle of the empty pail over his fingers.

"Now mind," said Mama, "don't you dare stick your finger in for a lick, or not a single molasses cookie will you have."

The sun was shining, and it was not a very cold day for the middle of January. Patrick ran as fast as he could to Mr. O'Connor's store.

When the storekeeper saw Patrick swinging the molasses pail, he shook his bald head. "Sorry I am to disappoint you, lad, but the

molasses barrel is empty. I'm getting a new barrel this afternoon. Come back after school, and I'll fill your pail."

Patrick walked slowly out of the store. His mouth was watering for molasses cookies hot from the oven. Then he had an idea. A few blocks farther on was another store—a bigger store. He had never gone there by himself, but he and Papa often passed it on their Sunday walks. The store was near the corner where they turned onto Commercial Street.

He did not have time to go home and ask Mama, but Patrick was sure he could get the molasses and not be late for school. Holding tight to the wire handle, Patrick ran lickety-split. He ran so hard that when he reached the store, he stopped on the doorstep to catch his breath.

At that very moment a heavy rumbling sound filled the air. BANG! BANG! BANG! BOOM! BOOM! WH-O-O-O-O-O-SH!

Patrick rushed to the corner. What he saw made his eyes bulge. A great, towering wave of smooth, shiny brown rolled toward him. It looked like … it looked like … IT WAS MOLASSES!

The Purity Distilling Company's huge, enormous tank had E-X-P-L-O-D-E-D!

People covered with molasses ran in all directions. People with their feet stuck fast screamed for help. Horses struggled in the sticky mess. Above all the noise and chaos, three long alarms sounded loudly through the streets.

WORD BANK

rumbling (RUM bling) *n.*: a deep, continuous, low sound that is like a soft thunder

chaos (KAY ahss) *n.*: complete confusion

All the while the river of molasses rolled toward
Patrick. Without stopping to think, he bent down by
the corner of the building. Grabbing the lid off his
pail, he held it out. The molasses poured into the pail,
nearly jerking it from Patrick's hands. He pulled it
back and clapped on the lid. The molasses spread up
the side street and lapped around Patrick's shoes.

Patrick turned to run, but he lost his footing in the gooey river. Down he went, his hand held tightly onto the pail. As he rolled over, a hand grabbed him.

"Are you all right, boy?" A man with hair as red as Patrick's smiled down at him. Strong hands pulled him to his feet.

Patrick nodded as he wiped his sticky face with a sticky hand. Before he could even say thank you, the man was gone. Patrick's shoes, his pants, his jacket, and his cap dripped with molasses. Patrick stamped off, stick—unstick, stick—unstick.

The terribly sweet smell of molasses filled the air. Around him men shouted, women screamed, and horses neighed. Behind him buildings crashed.

Patrick, however, did not look back. He was too busy licking molasses. Lick-lick. He licked first one hand then the other. Women called to him from their doorsteps. Patrick did not answer. With his thumb, Patrick wiped the molasses from his face. Lick-lick. He walked slowly on, the pail of molasses dangling from one hand. Stick—unstick, lick-lick. Stick—unstick, lick-lick.

Patrick ran his thumb over his jacket. Lick-lick. As he made his way home, Patrick became worried. Not only would Mama think he had taken a lick, but he was going to be late for school. Patrick knew he was in big trouble.

As Patrick started up the back walk, the kitchen door flew open. Mama stared at him. "Patrick McGonnigal O'Brien! What have you done to yourself?"

"I … I fell in the molasses, Mama." He gave his fingers a quick lick.

"What do you mean? 'Fell in the molasses.' You look as if you had climbed into Mr. O'Connor's barrel and licked it clean!" The red bun on Mama's head waggled back and forth.

Patrick shook his head. "Mr. O'Connor's barrel was empty, so I ran to the store near the corner of Commercial Street. Then I heard a terrible noise. BANG! BANG! BANG! BOOM! BOOM! WH-O-O-O-O-O-SH!" Patrick waved a sticky fist in the air.

"I ran to look. What do you think? The Purity Distilling Company's great big tank of molasses had popped open! The molasses rolled down the street right at me. I filled my pail and came home as fast as I could."

Mama's face turned bright red. "Patrick McGonnigal O'Brien! 'Tis bad enough that you are covered with molasses and late for school. Now you make matters worse by telling the silliest lie I ever heard!"

"It's true, Mama, every word!" cried Patrick. "I held out my bucket and filled it in the molasses river. If I hadn't fallen down …"

Mama grabbed him by the ear. "I never saw such a sticky mess nor heard such a tall tale. Come along and not another word out of you."

"But Mama …" Patrick cried.

"Patrick, I will hear no more stories, and I don't want you waking little Mary. I've had my hands full today already with your sister bumping her head and crying enough tears to make a flood."

"But Mama, there was a flood. A molasses flood."

"Patrick!"

Patrick sat in the big washtub in the middle of the kitchen floor. Every Saturday night he took his bath in it. This was not Saturday, but he was having a bath.

Mama's hands were not very gentle as she washed his hair and his neck and ears. "My goodness! There's even molasses on the back of your head. How did you ever get into such a sticky mess?"

Patrick tried again. "'Tis like I told you. The big tank of molasses over by Commercial Street ..."

Mama's eyes flashed like green lightning. "No more of that!" she scolded and rubbed him dry with a rough towel. She handed him his nightshirt. "It's into bed with you, and there you'll stay until you're ready to tell the truth."

Patrick opened his mouth and then shut it again. Mama was angrier than he had ever seen her. Angrier than the day he had spilled the molasses pitcher on the table. Patrick shook his head. He had told the truth, and she wouldn't believe him. Sadly he crawled into bed.

"Mind, when you're ready to tell what really happened, you can come out," said Mama as she closed the door.

Patrick pulled the covers up tight. He felt terrible. What could he say? He shut his eyes to think better. Soon he was fast asleep.

When Patrick awoke, he could smell supper cooking. He was hungry, but Mama had said … He rubbed his red hair. He would try again. He would start at the beginning and explain very slowly the way his teacher did. Patrick slid out of bed and tiptoed into the kitchen.

Mama was sitting at the table feeding Mary her porridge. Patrick stared at his sister. She had a bump on her forehead, half the size of a hen's egg. Mama looked at him sternly. "Are you ready to tell me what really happened?" she asked.

Patrick swallowed hard and nodded. "I took the molasses pail and went to Mr. O'Connor's store, just like you told me to do, Mama. But Mr. O'Connor's molasses barrel was empty." He took a deep breath. "So, I ran as fast as I could to the store near the corner of Commercial Street. I was sure I could fill my pail and not be late for school. Only … only …"

Patrick shook his head. He suddenly realized that if he had not seen that flood of molasses, he would not have believed it himself.

"Only what?" insisted Mama.

Patrick looked hard at his mother. "Mama, what would make a great big tank like that pop open?"

Mama shook her head. "It couldn't! That's why your story is so silly."

"But if it did," Patrick continued, "think what an awful mess it would make. Horses and people would get stuck in the molasses."

"Patrick, stop pretending, and tell me how you got in such a mess. Papa will soon be home, and …"

"Papa! I forgot about Papa!" Patrick's face turned white beneath his freckles. "I wonder where Papa was!"

"Papa? Papa's at …" Mama stopped short. Before she could say another word, the kitchen door opened, and Papa stepped in. At least Patrick thought it was Papa. From head to foot he was streaked with molasses. His face and hands were copper colored and his black hair and his clothes were all sticky. Papa closed the door behind him, and the heavy sweet smell of molasses filled the kitchen.

Mama gave a loud cry.

Papa stood there, trying to wipe a sticky hand on his sticky trousers. "Did you hear what happened?" he asked.

Mama just stared, as if she could not believe her eyes.

"The Purity Distilling Company tank exploded," said Papa, "and the tank was filled to the very top. Two million, three hundred and sixty thousand gallons of molasses poured out over the people, the buildings, and the streets."

Mama gasped, and her green eyes opened wider.

"I was sitting on the loading dock, eating my lunch," Papa went on. "All of a sudden I heard this terrible rumbling and shots that sounded like a giant machine gun being fired. Only it wasn't a gun. The rivets that hold the molasses tank together popped off like buttons off my jacket. The next thing I knew, one side of the tank had blown clear into the North Side Park. Fourteen thousand tons of molasses poured out, covering everything in its path—people, horses, wagons, cars, buildings, and even a piece of the raised train track."

Patrick looked at Mama. Would she tell Papa she didn't believe him and send him to bed? No. Mama was speechless.

Papa stuck out a sticky shoe. "Have you ever tried walking through molasses? It flowed into buildings and flooded basements. I worked all afternoon helping people and horses get unstuck. People from all over the city helped."

Papa rubbed a sticky ear. "It's a wonder you didn't hear the explosion way up here."

Mama shook her head weakly. "Oh dear, that must have been when Mary bumped her head. She set up such a howl." Mama looked from Papa to Patrick. "To think I wouldn't believe … Oh, Patrick, my boy! If you like, you can pour molasses all over your supper tonight."

Patrick drew a deep breath. The heavy smell of molasses filled his nose with a sickening sweetness. His tummy felt strange. "Thank you, Mama, but for once I've had all the molasses I want."

A Few Facts About Molasses

Molasses is a thick, sweet, sticky syrup, light to dark brown in color, that comes from sugar cane during the manufacture of sugar.

Molasses is mainly used in baking, candy making, and in feed for livestock.

Molasses has been an important product in New England since colonial times when it was shipped in from the West Indies and used to make rum.

Today, molasses is still widely used in Massachusetts in the making of Boston brown bread and Boston baked beans.

It Really

Oldtimers in Boston say that to this very day you can smell a faint whiff of molasses in the old buildings on Commercial Street. But is that only an oldtimer's tall tale?

The truth, as Patrick's mother would want to have it told, is that on January 15, 1919, a giant storage tank on Commercial Street in Boston's North End exploded. The tank, built by the Purity Distilling Company four years before, was filled with molasses, over 2,000,000 gallons.

When the tank popped, a great brown wave of molasses flooded downtown Boston, sweeping over everything in its path. In some places the molasses was three feet deep. Children on their lunch break from school were knocked over. Pieces of the tank flew in all directions, and one flying chunk of metal is reported to have crashed into the nearby freight house. Houses collapsed under the flood of molasses, and several people as well as horses were killed.

Rescue workers, trucks, and equipment had a difficult time getting through the streets of gooey liquid. Cleanup crews were brought in, but their task seemed almost impossible. Everywhere people walked

Happened

and everything they touched was sticky. Before the great flood ended, 21 people had been killed and 150 injured.

Even after the last brown glob disappeared from Commercial Street, the smell of molasses remained in Boston for a long time. Whether you can still sniff the molasses where it soaked into the cracks and crannies and under the wooden boards back in 1919, you will need to go to Boston and discover for yourself.

ABOUT THE AUTHOR

Both of **Marjorie Stover**'s parents were from families of Nebraska pioneers. Even though she was bored in history class in school, she always enjoyed hearing her family's historical stories. Mrs. Stover grew up to marry a history professor and write historical fiction. When she researches a story, she is fascinated by the little details. She finds out what people ate, how they dressed, and even how they talked. These details help her stories come alive.

The Grasshopper

The Grasshopper

David McCord

Down
a
deep
well
a
grasshopper
fell.

By kicking about
He thought to get out.
     He might have known better,
     For that got him wetter.
To kick round and round
Is the way to get drowned,
     And drowning is what
     I should tell you he got.
          But
          the
          well
          had
          a
          rope
          that
          dangled
          some
          hope.

And sure as molasses
On one of his passes
He found the rope handy
And up he went, *and he*
it
up
and
it
up
and
it
up
and
it
up
went
And hopped away proper
As any grasshopper.

Studying the Selection

QUICK REVIEW

1. In what city did Patrick live?

2. What did Patrick sometimes dream?

3. What was Mama's reaction when Patrick told her what had happened?

4. When did Mama find out the truth?

FOCUS

5. Why didn't Mama believe Patrick?

6. In historical fiction, some parts of the story are true and some are not. On a paper, write a T for true or an F for fiction for the following examples:

   a. The setting: Boston in the early 1900s.

   b. The plot: The explosion of a tank of molasses.

   c. The characters: Patrick and his family.

CREATING AND WRITING

7. Many people in Boston were affected by the explosion. Depending on where they were and what they were doing, they were affected in different ways. Pretend you are interviewing someone who experienced the explosion. Write down the questions and answers. Ask the person's name and age, and then ask several questions about where the person was during the explosion. Ask whether there was any injury or damage and any other interesting question you can think of. You should have at least three questions and answers in all.

8. Your teacher will divide the class into groups. Each group will be given one section of the story to pantomime, and a few minutes to prepare. Then, your teacher will call upon each group who will act out its part of the story. At the end, the class will have staged the entire story in pantomime.

Lesson in Literature ...

CREATING A SETTING

- Usually, either the plot or the characters are the most important element of a story. But sometimes, the main element is setting.

- When the main element is setting, the author will describe it in great detail.

- The best way to read this story is to use your imagination to picture the setting described.

- In addition to using your imagination to "see," you should use your imagination to hear, smell, and feel the sounds, smells, and objects described in the story.

THINK ABOUT IT!

1. Why was the kit fox especially hungry?

2. Why did the kit fox hunt for food during the day?

3. When the kit fox saw the rabbit on the highway, he had to choose between starvation and safety. Write one sentence to persuade the fox to get the rabbit, and one sentence to warn the fox to stay off the highway.

DESERT DANGER

The desert where the kit fox lived was very dry. The desert had had less than ten inches of rainfall the year before. Now it was even drier. It was so dry that there were even fewer animals than usual. The animals could not survive when the drought lasted so long. Even the desert plants, like cactus, were shriveled and dry.

The kit fox hunted at night. He would leave his underground den shortly after sunset. He was used to catching small animals such as kangaroo rats, rabbits, and prairie dogs. But food had recently been scarce, because the animals were scarce. They were scarce because they were starving. When he had been able to catch prey, it was usually insects and birds. This meant he needed more water. But the drought meant less water. He was so thirsty and so hungry.

The night before, he had gone looking for tomatoes and cactus fruits, but there were none to be found. He felt weak from lack of nourishment. How would he be able to flee from his enemies if he had no strength?

The animals he feared, the coyote and the red fox, were more likely to be out hunting during the night. So the kit fox came out of his den the next day. It was hardly cool in the burrow. The sun beating down was like the heavy beating of a drum.

He moved slowly in the direction of the highway. He feared the trucks and cars that sped noisily down the road. They were big and released bad smells. But maybe there would be water or prey to be found nearby.

He reached the steaming blacktop. He would have to be careful to look up for oncoming vehicles. Even with the fur on the bottom of his paws, it felt like the tar of the road was boiling. He crossed quickly.

As he neared the other side, he spied a dead rabbit in the farthest lane. It had been hit by a car. He ran faster and clamped his jaw on the nape of the rabbit's neck. He began to drag it in the direction of home. When he had almost reached the other side of the road, a tractor trailer came barreling down.

The kit fox could not lose the rabbit. He was hungry and thirsty. He hadn't had meat in such a long time. The rabbit would also quench his thirst. The tractor trailer came closer and closer. The kit fox made it off the road just in time. Then he collapsed in the shade of some brush. He was exhausted. He felt he could not move. As he lay there, he could feel the hard ground under his body.

He clutched the dead rabbit in his paws and chewed a little. He would not make it to his den without being chased by his enemies. He needed to eat enough to get the energy to race to his den dragging the rabbit in his mouth.

As he rested and ate, he gathered strength. Time passed. Then he picked up the remains of the rabbit and raced for home.

Blueprint for Reading

INTO . . . *Bear Mouse*

Living things are all around us. Mosquitoes hum in our ears; ants crawl on the ground; birds, squirrels, and rabbits all go about their business, scurrying here and there looking for food, building nests, and feeding their young. What would it be like to be one of them? How would it feel to always be hunting for food or on the lookout for enemies? As you read *Bear Mouse*, you will see the world from the eyes of a cold and hungry mouse, who wants only a few seeds to eat and a warm nest for her family.

EYES ON *Setting As the Most Important Element*

Everyone has experiences that stand out in their minds. Sometimes, they remember an unusual adventure. In a story, that would be called the *plot*. Sometimes, they remember meeting somebody new who was very interesting and unusual. In a story, that would be called the *main character*. Sometimes, they remember a place they visited. In a story, that would be called the *setting*. The most important element of most stories is either the plot or the main character. In *Bear Mouse*, the plot and characters are very simple, but the setting is memorable. As you read *Bear Mouse*, try to *be* the mouse, and feel her cold, and her fright, and her hunger. If you do, you will not easily forget this story.

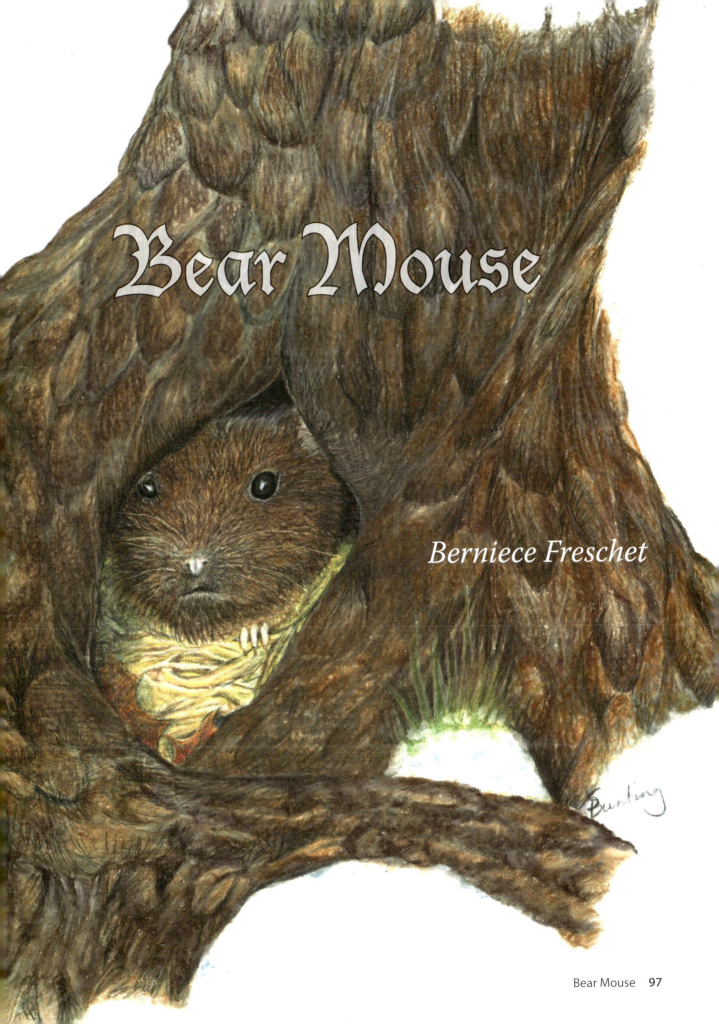

Bear Mouse

Berniece Freschet

The snow was deep. A quilt of white covered the meadow. It piled high against a stone wall. Branches on the pine and birch bent low.

Under the soft quilt, a meadow mouse, shaggy as a little bear, ran down a snow tunnel. Her path crossed another. She quickly turned, following along the new mouse-trail.

There were many of these snowy tunnels rambling through the meadow—a network of trails that crossed and crossed again. They were worn smooth by the constant running of tiny mouse-feet.

WORD BANK

constant (KAHN stunt) *adj.*: continuing without a stop

Suddenly the little mouse stopped. She sat up on her hind legs. She sat very still. Every muscle in her small body was tense.

She had many enemies to look out for! What had she heard? A gray squirrel …. Or the soft, padded paws of a weasel overhead? The red fox slinking near? Or did she sense that the weasel and the bobcat were out on the hunt for a dinner of mouse, watching for the smallest telltale movement in the snow.

Her small ears, almost hidden under her coarse fur, listened for the smallest sound. She flicked an ear, brushing it against the tunnel wall.

She heard the musical tinkling of snow-crystals falling. Then all was quiet. Soon she hurried on, down the trail.

WORD BANK

telltale (TELL tale) *adj.*: something that *tells* (reveals) something that would not be known otherwise

Another meadow mouse ran toward her. For a minute they stopped, their noses twitching … touching. They pushed past each other. Then off they ran in opposite directions, each intent on getting to somewhere.

A minute later the mouse pushed into an opening. Down she went to her nest in a tangle of twisted roots.

It was a good place, cozy and warm. In the middle of the nest, close together on a soft bed of dry grasses, lay four tiny mouse-babies. They smelled their mother's nearness. They squeaked their hunger. The tiny mice wanted their dinner. But there was little milk for the week-old babies.

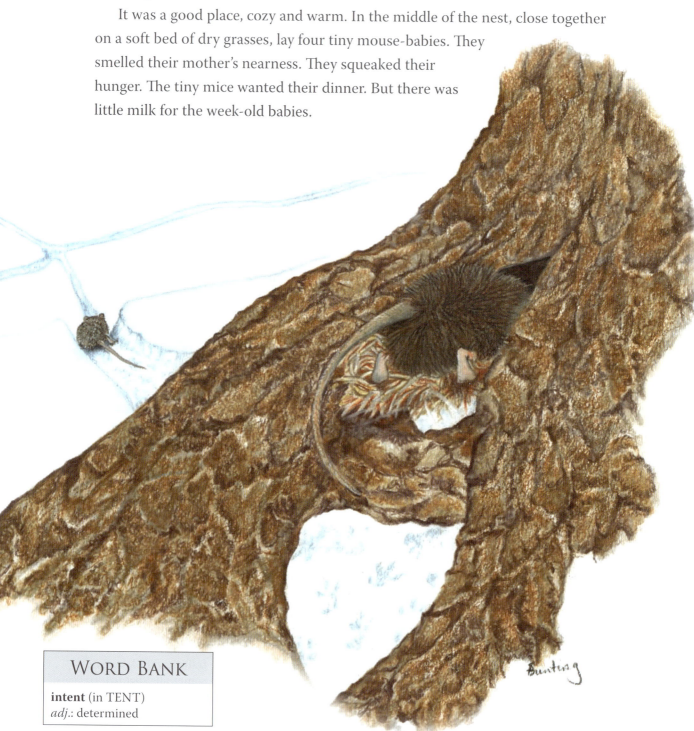

WORD BANK

intent (in TENT)
adj.: determined

During her last hunt, the meadow mouse had found only one dried hazelnut to eat. This was not enough food to make the milk to feed her hungry young.

Gently the mother mouse pushed her nose into the soft mound of fur. Her pink tongue licked each tiny mouse-baby. She chirruped[1] soft sounds of comfort.

But the mouse knew she could not stay long. She must find something more to eat.

In jerky movements, she circled her babies. Then with one last quick turn, she left the nest, hurrying off down a snow tunnel. She moved into a trail that led upward. Soon she popped her head out of the snow.

---

1. A *chirrup* is a chirp, a short, sharp sound.

She looked around. Her black, shiny eyes watched for signs of danger. All seemed safe. The little mouse came out of her tunnel. She ran to the foot of an old pine tree.

Sunlight sparkled on the white snow. There was a sudden flash of red as a cardinal flew out of the tree and swooped away across the meadow.

The mouse sat up, and with her front paws, she carefully cleaned the snow from her coat of fur. She looked different from most other kinds of mice.

Instead of a narrow pointed head, her head was round. Instead of a sleek, smooth body, hers was chunky. She had small ears and a hairy tail. Her legs were short. Her long, dark-brown hair made her legs seem even shorter. Because of her shaggy coat of fur, she looked like a "bear mouse."

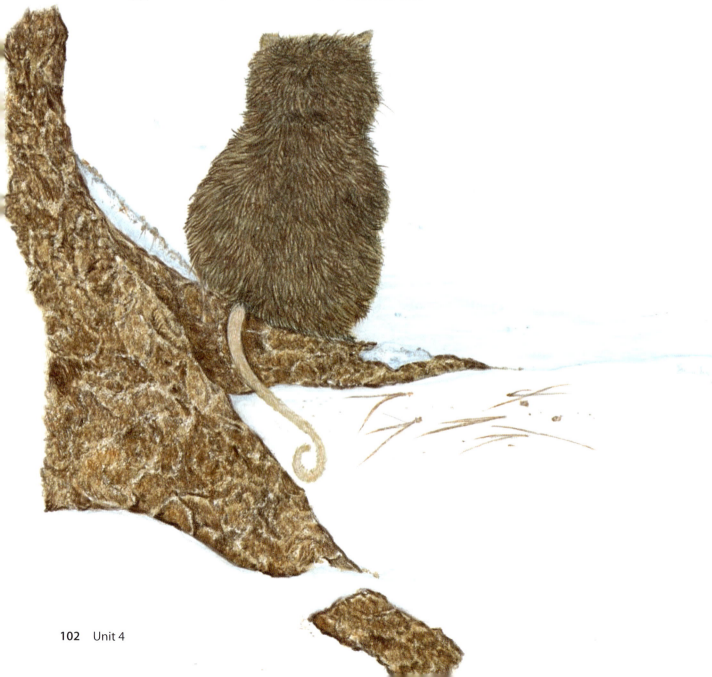

The little meadow mouse was very hungry.

In the summer, when food was plentiful, she liked to eat seeds, roots, and berries. Her favorite food was sweet clover, and tender plants of alfalfa. But now the snow was deep and food was hard to find. Winter had come early this year. The mouse's storehouse of seeds was already gone.

She stuck her nose into a crack in the tree. She was looking for a bite of something—a weed seed, or maybe a dry tuft of moss. But she found nothing. She often visited the old pine tree. She had long ago picked it clean of every seed, every nut, every dry blade of grass.

High above in the blue sky, a hawk flew over the meadow. He swooped down. The black shadow of his wings skimmed across the white snow.

Quietly, nearer he flew.

The meadow mouse sat very still.

She sensed danger. The hawk dipped low. Sharp talons opened wide.

With a squeak, the mouse dived into the snow. She ran down a tunnel. Soon she stopped and crouched against the snow-path to rest.

She listened. Except for the wild beating of her heart, all was still.

When her fear passed, she hurried on. She came to a path that led up to the pond. Maybe she would find something to eat there. Up she climbed.

WORD BANK
skimmed *v*.: passed over lightly
talons (TA lunz) *n*.: claws
crouched (KROWCHD) *v*.: stooped low to the ground

WORD BANK

hibernation (HI ber NAY shun) *n.:* the act of sleeping through the winter months

burrowed (BURR ode) *v.:* living in a hole dug deep in the ground

Turtle Pond was frozen over. Winter's quiet had come to the pond. The songbirds were gone. Many creatures were in hibernation, sleeping away the long, cold months.

The duck family who made their home here in the summer had flown to a warmer land. And the playful otters had long ago left for the big river.

The old bullfrog, the water snake, and the turtles were asleep. They were burrowed deep in the mud at the bottom of the pond.

Only the bigmouth bass and a few water creatures still swam under their roof of ice.

At the edge of the pond the mouse hunted for a snail. She looked for a water bug that might be caught in the snow. But the sparrows had already found and snapped up the trapped insects. There were no snails here, only two dry shells.

The mouse's stomach felt very empty. She licked at the snow. She darted under an alder bush and looked for an extra leaf or two that might still be hanging there. But the bush was bare, eaten clean by the deer. There was something else though …

A cocoon hanging from a stem. Food!

darted (DART ed) *v*.: started suddenly and ran swiftly

cocoon (kuh KOON) *n*.: a silky case in which certain insects enclose their eggs

Quickly the mouse ran up the stem. Holding the cocoon in her front paws, she ate it all. When she was finished, she ran under the low-hanging branches of a small spruce tree. Here she sat, cleaning her whiskers.

She felt better now, but she was still hungry. Soon out she dashed, running for the stone wall at the side of the meadow. She left behind her a trail of footprints in the soft snow.

The sun was low in the sky. The mouse would have to return to her babies soon. But first she needed more to eat. She had to find food to make milk for her young, or they would starve.

Overhead the cardinal flashed by. Something dropped from his bill. A red holly berry lay in the snow. The mouse hurried toward it. It was dangerous for her to be out in the open. But hunger made the mouse forget caution. She picked up the berry and began to eat it.

High in the old pine tree, a snowy owl looked out across the still, white meadow. He spread his great wings and sailed up and up.

"Whooo-whoo-whoo-" he called softly.

The little mouse heard the hunting cry of the owl. She darted for the safety of the stone wall. She crouched, waiting. Her small body shook with fear and hunger.

A snowshoe rabbit crouched near—one long ear bending forward. Quickly, in zigzagging leaps he ran away, hurrying for safe cover in the blackberry bushes.

For a while the mouse stayed close to the stone wall. But now she was more and more troubled. She had been away from her nest for too long. Even though she had not found food, she must return to her babies. The little mouse started across the meadow.

Suddenly she stopped. A strange, wild scent filled the air. The little mouse stood high. She looked around. She turned her head to one side and then to the other. Her ears twisted this way and that. She listened for the smallest sound. She sniffed the air.

At the edge of the meadow, a bobcat slunk low. He crept forward, toward the mouse.

Slowly, nearer and nearer crept the bobcat.

Now he was close enough.

He pounced!

The mouse leaped to one side. Again the bobcat sprang! The mouse dodged to the other side.

Twisting and turning, the little mouse raced for the safety of the stone wall. The cat was at her heels. She was almost to the wall. With a great bound, the bobcat leaped forward—

The mouse felt sharp claws rake her fur. End over end, she somersaulted across the snow.

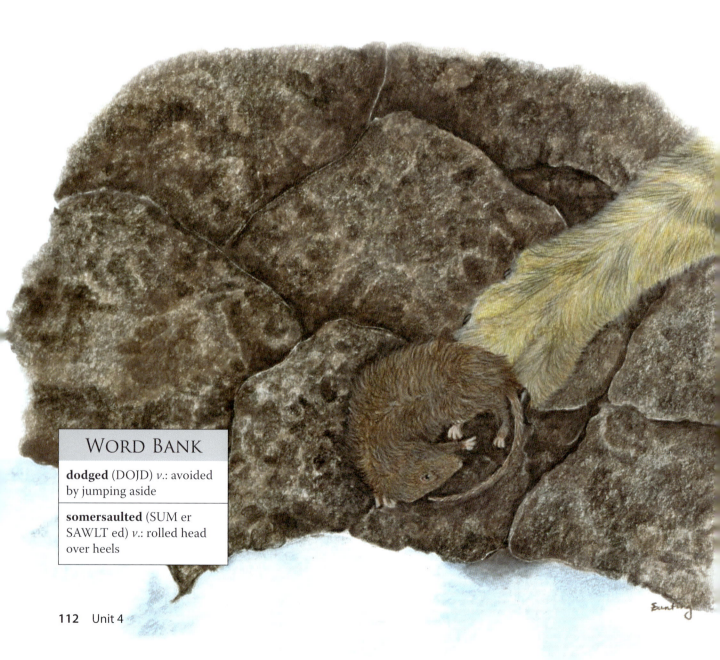

Word Bank

dodged (DOJD) *v.*: avoided by jumping aside

somersaulted (SUM er SAWLT ed) *v.*: rolled head over heels

In a last, desperate leap, the mouse sprang for the wall. She squeezed herself into a crack between the stones.

The cat pushed a paw inside. His sharp claws stretched toward the mouse, but he could not reach her. The little mouse was safe.

With an angry snarl the bobcat turned and trotted away to look for his supper at the pond.

Her close escape and her hunger had worn out the mouse. Her strength was almost gone. She was too weak now to return to her nest and her young.

WORD BANK

desperate (DESS prut) *adj.*: done because of tremendous need

She lay huddled against a rock, her small sides heaving. She rested. She ate a dry tuft of grass stuck between the stones. It was not much but it helped to fill her empty stomach. With her forepaws she pulled at the grass.

Suddenly, out of the crack between the stones, spilled acorns and weed seeds. It was a squirrel's forgotten storehouse of food.

Today the little mouse was lucky.

She ate and ate until her small stomach could not hold one seed more. Then she stuffed her cheeks full. Away she raced—back to her tunnels in the snow. She raced back to her nest and her family.

With tiny squeaks of delight, the mouse-babies welcomed their mother. She pulled them close. When their stomachs were stretched tight with the warm milk, the mouse-babies snuggled into their mother's shaggy fur. Safe and warm in their cozy nest, the mouse-family went to sleep.

ABOUT THE AUTHOR

Berniece Freschet wrote 27 children's books about the animals of her native Montana. She became an author while raising her five children. Her daughter, Gina, recalls spending hours in the library with her mother while Mrs. Freschet was researching for her books. Gina followed in her mother's footsteps, and today, she too is an author, as well as an illustrator. She even illustrated a few of her mother's books! Besides for writing, Mrs. Freschet enjoyed reading, traveling, music, and camping.

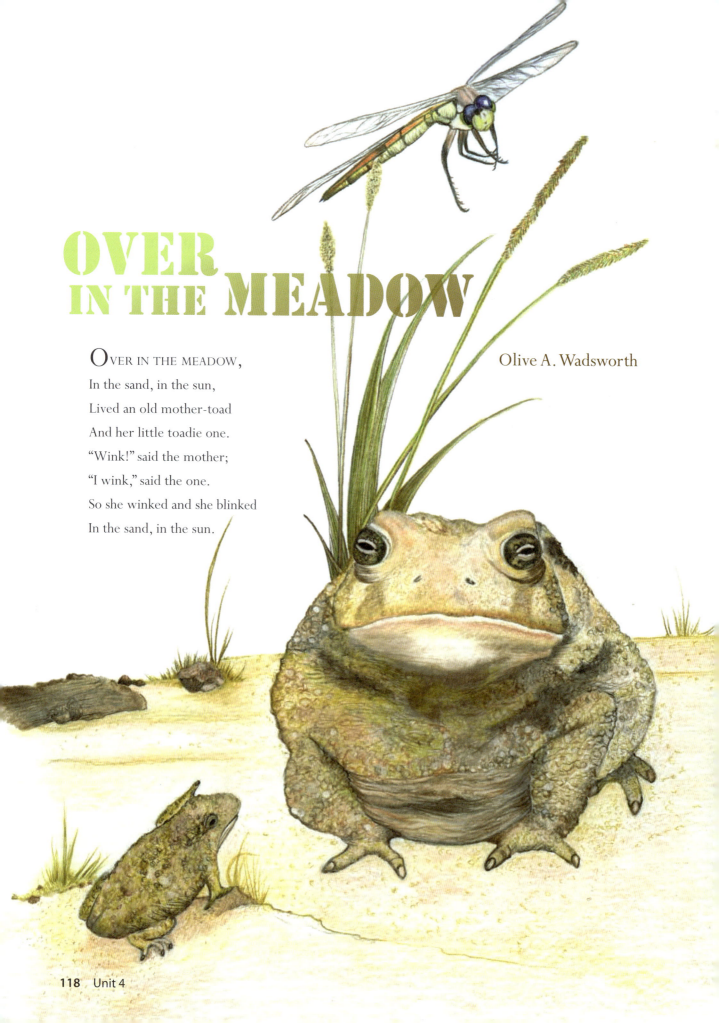

OVER IN THE MEADOW

Olive A. Wadsworth

OVER IN THE MEADOW,
In the sand, in the sun,
Lived an old mother-toad
And her little toadie one.
"Wink!" said the mother;
"I wink," said the one.
So she winked and she blinked
In the sand, in the sun.

OVER IN THE MEADOW,
Where the stream runs blue,
Lived an old mother-fish
And her little fishes two.
"Swim!" said the mother;
"We swim," said the two.
So they swam and they leaped
Where the stream runs blue.

OVER IN THE MEADOW,
In a hole in a tree,
Lived an old mother-bluebird
And her little birdies three.
"Sing!" said the mother;
"We sing," said the three.
So they sang and were glad
In the hole in the tree.

Over in the meadow,
In the reeds on the shore,
Lived an old mother-muskrat
And her little ratties four.
"Dive!" said the mother;
"We dive," said the four.
So they dived and they burrowed
In the reeds on the shore.

OVER IN THE MEADOW,
In a snug beehive,
Lived a mother-honeybee
And her little bees five.
"Buzz!" said the mother;
"We buzz," said the five.
So they buzzed and they hummed
In the snug beehive.

Over in the meadow,
In a nest built of sticks,
Lived a black mother-crow
And her little crows six.
"Caw!" said the mother;
"We caw," said the six.
So they cawed and they called
In the nest built of sticks.

Over in the meadow,
Where the grass is so even,
Lived a gray mother-cricket
and her little crickets seven.
"Chirp!" said the mother;
"We chirp," said the seven.
So they chirped cheery notes
In the grass soft and even.

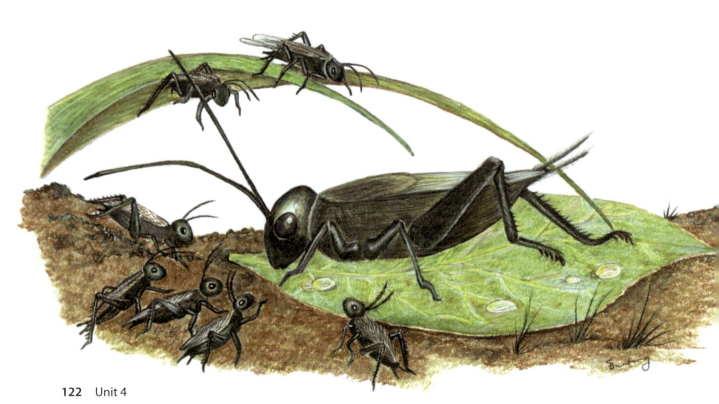

Over in the meadow,
By the old mossy gate,
Lived a brown mother-lizard
And her little lizards eight.
"Bask!" said the mother;
"We bask," said the eight.
So they basked in the sun
By the old mossy gate.

Over in the meadow,
Where the clear pools shine,
Lived a green mother-frog
And her little froggies nine.
"Croak!" said the mother;
"We croak," said the nine.
So they croaked and they splashed
Where the clear pools shine.

Over in the meadow,
In a sly little den,
Lived a gray mother-spider
And her little spiders ten.
"Spin!" said the mother;
"We spin," said the ten.
So they spun lace webs
In the sly little den.

Studying the Selection

FIRST IMPRESSIONS

What does the world look like to a cold and hungry meadow mouse? Where will she find food out in the cold snow? Will she be able to hide from all her enemies? Her poor, starving babies are counting on her. Will she return safely to her nest?

QUICK REVIEW

1. How did the little mouse move around under the snow?

2. What were four different enemies that the mouse had to fear?

3. When the mouse reached the pond, what did she find?

4. What food did the mouse finally eat?

FOCUS

5. The little mouse possessed some qualities from which people could learn. She was courageous, persistent, and loving. Write three sentences that explain how you know the mouse had these qualities. In your first sentence explain how she was courageous. In the second sentence explain how she was persistent. In the third sentence explain how she was loving.

6. Although the story describes the setting above the ground, the mouse's nest is only briefly described. What do you think it looked and felt like? Imagine that you are a baby mouse. Using words that describe the way things look, feel, smell, and sound, describe the nest from your point of view.

CREATING AND WRITING

7. Write a short story about the same meadow mouse hunting for food. She will go to the same places and face the same enemies. This time, though, it is summer. Your story should be two to three paragraphs long.

8. Using art materials distributed by your teacher, your class will create a display that includes the mouse, the snow, the frozen pond, and all the mouse's enemies described in the story. Your teacher will assign different parts of the display to different students.

4 unit

The Town That Moved

Heartland

No Laughing Matter

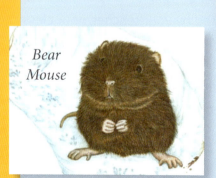

Bear Mouse

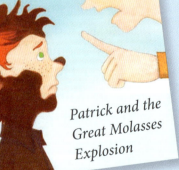

Patrick and the Great Molasses Explosion

Imagine that you are designing a maze for Euclid Beach Park called "Bear Mouse Maze." People enter the maze on foot and try to find the path that will lead them to the exit. When they are on the right path, they will see colorful pictures of food and shelter. If they are on the wrong path, they will reach a dead end with a scary picture of something that is dangerous for Bear Mouse. They will have to turn around and try to find the right path.

Look through the story and choose three of the dangers that Bear Mouse faced. Your teacher will give you three pieces of construction paper. On each piece of paper, draw a picture of one of those dangers and print the words: Wrong Way! Beware of _____. (Fill in the name of the danger you are drawing.)

ACTIVITY ONE

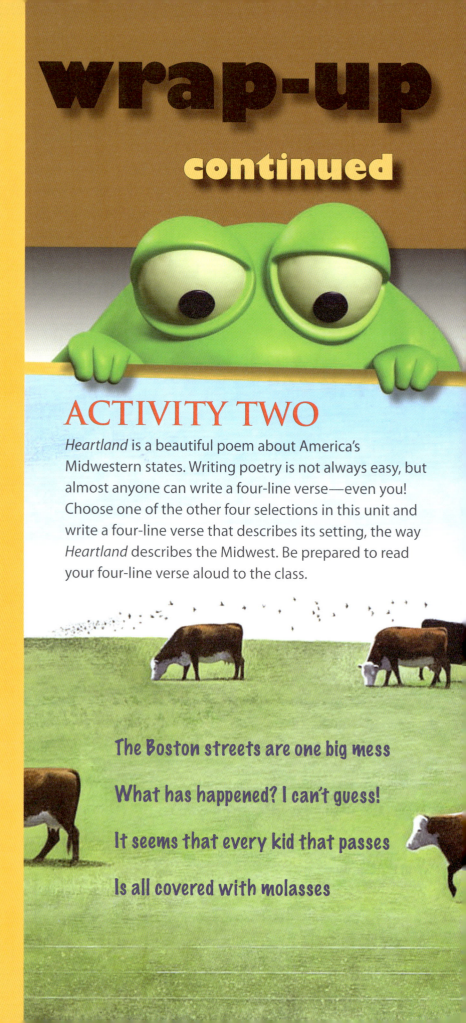

ACTIVITY TWO

Heartland is a beautiful poem about America's Midwestern states. Writing poetry is not always easy, but almost anyone can write a four-line verse—even you! Choose one of the other four selections in this unit and write a four-line verse that describes its setting, the way *Heartland* describes the Midwest. Be prepared to read your four-line verse aloud to the class.

The Boston streets are one big mess

What has happened? I can't guess!

It seems that every kid that passes

Is all covered with molasses

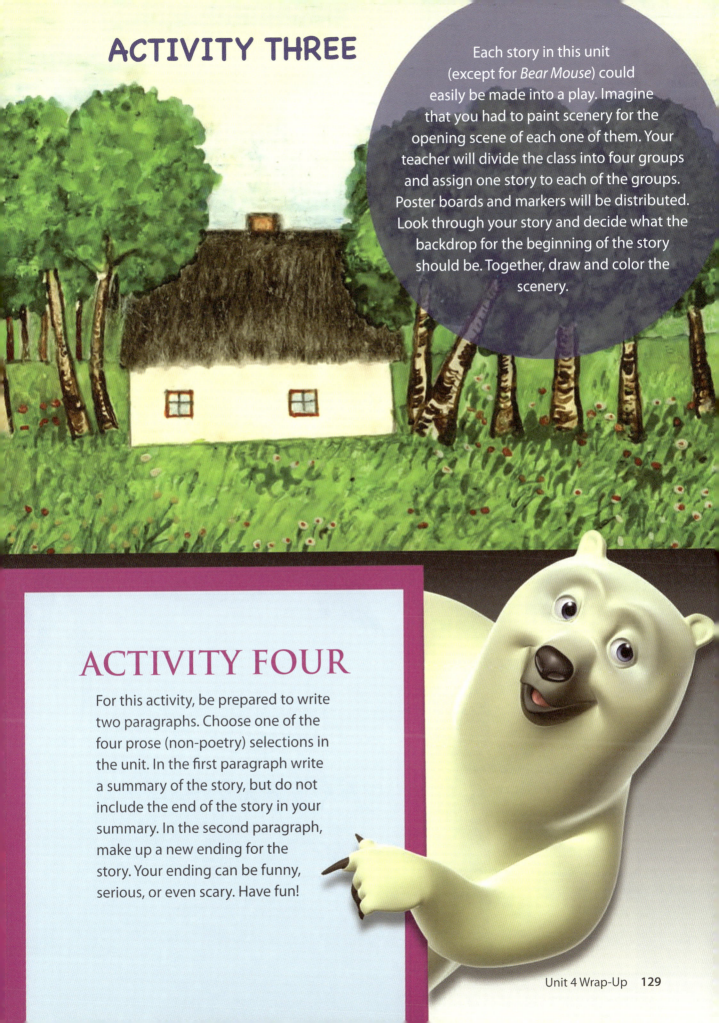

ACTIVITY THREE

Each story in this unit (except for *Bear Mouse*) could easily be made into a play. Imagine that you had to paint scenery for the opening scene of each one of them. Your teacher will divide the class into four groups and assign one story to each of the groups. Poster boards and markers will be distributed. Look through your story and decide what the backdrop for the beginning of the story should be. Together, draw and color the scenery.

ACTIVITY FOUR

For this activity, be prepared to write two paragraphs. Choose one of the four prose (non-poetry) selections in the unit. In the first paragraph write a summary of the story, but do not include the end of the story in your summary. In the second paragraph, make up a new ending for the story. Your ending can be funny, serious, or even scary. Have fun!

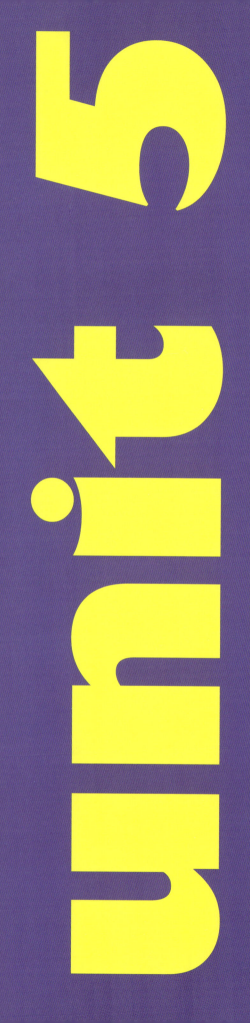

unit 5

SYMPATHY

GIVING

FRIENDSHIP

all about theme!

Lesson in Literature...

THE CHILDREN'S HOME

WHAT IS AUTHOR'S PURPOSE?

- The reason an author writes a story is called the **author's purpose**.

- An author may write a story simply to entertain the reader. For this purpose, the author may write a comedy, a mystery, or an adventure story.

- An author may wish to inform the reader of something. For this purpose, the author may write a piece of nonfiction or historical fiction.

- An author may write a story to express ideas or emotions. For this purpose, the author could write any kind of fiction or nonfiction.

THINK ABOUT IT!

1. How did John treat David?
2. How did David feel when John was adopted?
3. What idea did the author want to express at the end of the story?

David lived in a children's home on East 7th Street in New York's Lower East Side. The buildings were old, but it wasn't bad there. The food wasn't so good, but they had enough to eat. There were 25 boys in each dormitory. David's bed was next to John's. John was his best friend.

It was good to have a best friend. A tall iron fence surrounded the buildings, which separated them from the neighborhood. The only time the boys left the children's home was when they attended school, P.S. 25. The teachers and the other students tried to include them in all their activities, but the boys from the home always felt different.

Then the children's home moved to Yonkers, in the country. John told David that it was going to be a lot nicer there. In fact, outside it was nothing like the city. There were orchards of apple and pear trees, woodlands, and meadows. Even though the dormitories were much larger, with 105 beds, David and John's beds were still side by side.

John was like an older brother to David. He taught him how to play baseball in the fields at the new children's home. He read books to

David. With the bigger library at Yonkers, he was able to introduce David to new authors. John gave David a love of reading. The boys spent all their free moments together.

One day, John received a letter from a cousin he didn't know he had. His cousin said that he had been trying to track him down for nearly a year. John read the weekly letters to David. Then John's cousin wrote and said he and his wife would visit on Sunday.

Sunday came. John dressed in his best shirt and pants. John was out on his visit for several hours. David tried to read but couldn't concentrate. Usually, Sunday afternoon was a time he spent with John. He was very lonely. When John came back to the dorm, he showed David the new clothes his family had left him. His cousin's wife had baked brownies for him. He gave David half of his brownies.

Several weeks passed and the weekly letters continued. Then the director called John to his office. "Your cousin and his wife would like to adopt you. What do you think of that?" John said quietly, "Maybe that would be wonderful."

When John told David, David asked, "Does that mean you will go away?" John nodded. "I'll leave in a few weeks, probably."

David stopped speaking to John. What was the point of speaking if he were leaving? John was the only person who had ever cared about him. How could he live without John?

John tried to talk with David many times each day. Then the day came when he left. David felt like a hole had opened up in his heart. It seemed to be more than he could endure.

Three months passed. John's bed was still empty. Then one night, a new boy was there. The boy said, "Hi. My name is Sam." David was silent. He looked Sam up and down. Sam was just a kid, maybe seven years old. David started to turn away.

He didn't know why, but he turned back around. "My name is David." David thought of John. David was much younger than he. John had given him so much!

David reached out his hand and said, "Hey, we're neighbors. Let's shake on it!" They shook on it.

"You want me to read you a story before we go to sleep?" Tears ran down Sam's cheeks and he nodded yes.

Blueprint for Reading

INTO . . . *A Gift for Tía Rosa*

Have you ever heard the word *bittersweet*? It means just what
it says: it is something that is both bitter and sweet, all at the
same time. *A Gift for Tía Rosa* is like that. It is about something
very sweet—the love between a little girl and a warm, wonderful
woman. But when two people love each other, there is always
the chance that they may be separated. Then there is a struggle
between the sweet feelings of the past and the sad feelings of the
present. Which will win out? As you read *A Gift for Tía Rosa*, try to
understand all the different ways Carmela felt, and guess how she
will feel as time goes by.

EYES ON *Author's Purpose*

Have you ever read a story and wondered: Why did the author
write this? What was the **author's purpose**? Well, why would *you*
write a story? Perhaps you're a good entertainer, and you like
telling people stories that are funny or unusual. Perhaps you're
a good teacher, and you want to teach an audience something
you think they should know. Then again, maybe you're the kind of
person who enjoys sharing feelings and thoughts with others, and
you've reacted to an experience in a way that you really want to
share. The author's purpose may be to entertain, to inform, or to
express feelings. Many times, an author will write a story for two,
or even all three, of these reasons. As you read *A Gift for Tía Rosa*,
ask yourself: What was the author's purpose in writing this story?

A GIFT FOR TÍA ROSA

KAREN T. TAHA

"Around, over, through, and pull. Around, over, through, and pull," Carmela[1] repeated as she knitted. A rainbow of red, orange, and gold wool stretched almost to her feet. Now and then she stopped and listened for her father's car. He mustn't see what she was knitting!

The rumble of a motor made her drop the needles and run to the window. In the gray November shadows, she saw a battered brown station wagon turn into the garage next door.

"Mamá, she's home! Tía[2] Rosa is home!" Carmela called. Carmela's mother hurried out of the bedroom. She put her arm around Carmela. They watched as lights flickered on in the windows, bringing the neat white house back to life.

"I know you want to see Tía Rosa, Carmela," said her mother, "but she and Tío Juan[3] have had a long trip. Tía Rosa must be very tired after two weeks in the hospital."

"But can I call her, Mamá?" asked Carmela. "The scarf for Papá is almost done. She promised to help me fringe it when she came home."

<table>
<tr><td>

WORD BANK

flickered (FLIK erd) *v.*: shone with a wavering light

fringe (FRINJ) *v.*: to make a fringe, a border of loose threads at the end of a scarf or shawl

</td></tr>
</table>

---

1. *Carmela* (kar MELL lah)
2. *Tía* (TEE ah) is Spanish for "aunt."
3. *Tío Juan* (TEE o WAHN) is Spanish for "Uncle Juan."

"No, Carmela. Not now," her mother replied firmly. "Tía Rosa needs to rest." She smoothed back Carmela's thick black hair from her face.

Carmela tossed her head. "But Mamá …!"

"No, Carmela!"

Carmela knew there was no use arguing. But it wasn't fair. Tomorrow she would have to go to school. She couldn't see Tía Rosa until the afternoon. Her mother just didn't understand.

Frowning, Carmela plopped back on the sofa and picked up the silver knitting needles. At least she would finish more of the scarf before Tía Rosa saw it tomorrow. She bent over her knitting and began once more. "Around, over, through, and pull." The phone rang in the kitchen.

"I'll get it!" Carmela shouted, bounding into the hall. "Hello?" Her dark eyes sparkled. "Tía Rosa! You must see Papá's scarf. It's almost finished … You did? For me? Okay, I'll be right there!"

The phone clattered as Carmela hung up. "Mamá! Tía Rosa wants to see the scarf. She even brought me a surprise!"

Carmela's mother smiled and shook her head. "Tía Rosa is unbelievable."

Carmela stuffed the bright wool into her school bag. "I'm going to make Tía Rosa a surprise after I finish Papá's scarf!" she called as she ran out.

She ran across the yard to Tía Rosa's front door. The door swung open, and there was Tío Juan. He looked taller and thinner than she remembered, and his eyes looked sad.

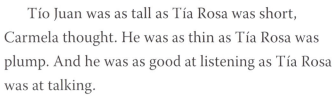

Tío Juan was as tall as Tía Rosa was short, Carmela thought. He was as thin as Tía Rosa was plump. And he was as good at listening as Tía Rosa was at talking.

"*Hola*,[4] Carmelita," he said, bending to kiss her cheek. He led her down the hall. "Tía Rosa is sitting up in bed. She's tired, but she wanted to see her favorite neighbor."

Tía Rosa in bed! In all her eight years Carmela had never seen Tía Rosa sick. She held her breath and peeked into the bedroom. Tía Rosa's round face crinkled into a smile when she saw Carmela.

4. *Hola* (O lah) is Spanish for "hello."

"Carmelita, come give me a hug!"

Hugging Tía Rosa always made Carmela feel safe and warm. Tía Rosa was like a soft pillow that smelled of soap and bath powder and sometimes of sweet tamales.[5] Now there was another smell, a dentist office smell, Carmela decided.

"Carmelita, I've missed you!" said Tía Rosa. "Let's look at what you have knitted."

Carmela handed her the scarf. Tía Rosa smiled. "Your papá will be proud to wear it," she said. "Tomorrow I'll show you how to fringe it, and I will start on the pink baby blanket for my granddaughter!"

Carmela laughed. "How do you know that Pepe's wife will have a girl?" she asked. Pepe was the oldest of Tía Rosa's six sons.

"Because," answered Tía Rosa with a grin, "anyone who has six sons and no daughters, deserves a granddaughter!"

"But Tía Rosa, what if the baby is a boy? Won't you love him just the same?"

"Of course," laughed Tía Rosa.

Carmela knew Tía Rosa would love the baby, boy or girl, but she wished for a girl, too.

---

5. *Tamales* (tah MAH lis) are a Mexican dish in which chopped meat is packed into cornmeal dough, wrapped in corn husks, and steamed.

"Now for the surprise!" said Tía Rosa. She handed Carmela a small white box. "Go on now. See what's inside."

Carmela opened the box carefully. A snowy ball of cotton lay inside. As she pulled at the cotton, her fingers touched something hard and very small. She heard the "clish" of a chain as she lifted the surprise from under the cotton. In her hand Carmela held a tiny silver rose on a fine chain.

"Oh, Tía Rosa. It's beautiful!" exclaimed Carmela.

"The rose is so you'll remember your old Tía Rosa," she said.

"How could I forget you, Tía Rosa?" asked Carmela. "You're right here!"

Before she went home, Carmela put the rose around her neck. She promised to return the next day after school.

Carmela returned the next day, and the next, and every day for a whole week. Tía Rosa stayed in her room, and Tío Juan moved a chair by the bed for Carmela. Together the two friends worked on their surprise gifts.

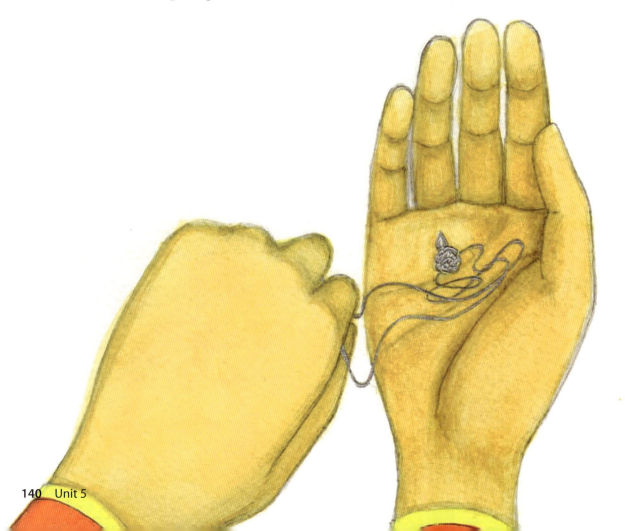

"Why does Tía Rosa stay in bed all the time?" Carmela asked her father at breakfast one day.

Her father looked away for a moment. Then he took Carmela's hands in his. "Tía Rosa is very sick, Carmela. The doctors don't think she can get well," he explained.

"But Papá," said Carmela. "I have been sick lots of times. Remember when Tía Rosa stayed with me when you and Mamá had to go away?"

"Yes," answered her father. "But Tía Rosa …"

Carmela didn't listen. "Now I will stay with Tía Rosa until she gets well, too," she said.

Every afternoon Carmela worked on her father's scarf. The fringe was the easiest part. With Tía Rosa's help she would have the scarf finished long before the holidays.

Tía Rosa worked on the pink baby blanket, but the needles didn't fly in her sure brown fingers like they once did. Carmela teased her. "Tía Rosa, are you knitting slowly because you might have to change the pink yarn to blue when the baby is born?"

"No, no," replied Tía Rosa with a grin. "The baby will surely be a girl. We need girls in this family. You're the only one I have!"

Sometimes Tía Rosa fell asleep with her knitting still in her hands. Then Carmela would quietly put the needles and yarn into Tía Rosa's big green knitting bag and tiptoe out of the room.

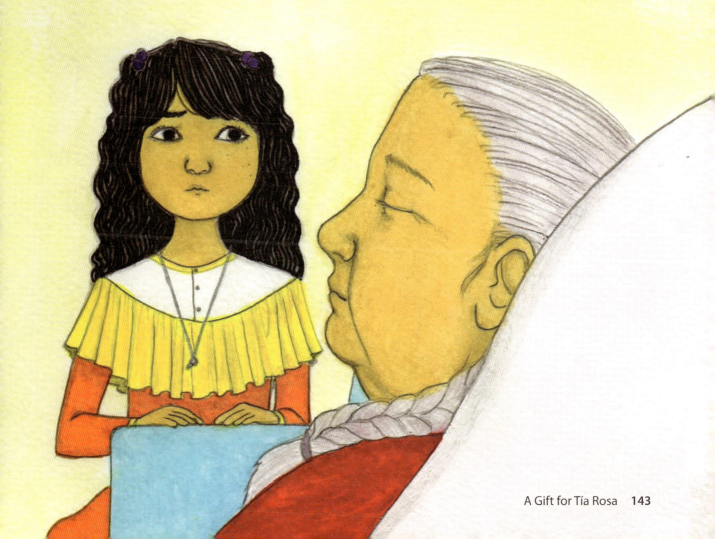

Carmela liked Saturdays and Sundays best because she could spend more time at Tía Rosa's. Mamá always sent a plate of cookies with her, and Tío Juan made hot chocolate for them.

One Saturday morning when Carmela rang the doorbell, Tío Juan didn't come. Carmela ran to the garage and peeked in the window. The brown station wagon was gone.

She returned home and called Tía Rosa's number. The phone rang and rang. Carmela went down the steps to the basement. Her mother was rubbing stain into the freshly sanded wood of an old desk.

"Tía Rosa isn't home," said Carmela sadly. Her mother looked up from her work.

"I thought I heard a car in the night," said her mother. "Surely Tío Juan would have called us if …"

Just then the phone rang upstairs.
Carmela heard footsteps creak across the
floor as her father walked to answer it.

Moments later the footsteps thumped
softly towards the basement door.
Carmela's father came slowly down the
steps. Carmela shivered when she saw
his sad face. He put his arms around

Carmela and her mother and hugged them close. "Tía Rosa is gone," he whispered. "She died early this morning."

No, her father's words couldn't be true. Carmela didn't believe it. Tía Rosa would come back. She had always come back before.

"It's not true!" cried Carmela. She broke away from her mother and father and raced up the stairs. She ran out the front door and through the

yard to Tía Rosa's house. She pushed the doorbell again and again. She pounded on the silent door until her fists hurt. At last she sank down on the steps.

Later her father came. With a soft hanky he brushed the tears from her cheeks. At last they walked quietly home.

The next days were long and lonely for Carmela. She didn't care that Papá's finished scarf lay hidden in her closet, bright and beautiful. She didn't want to see it. She didn't want to feel the cool, smooth knitting needles in her hands ever again.

The white house next door was busy with people coming and going. Carmela took over food her mother and father cooked, but she quickly returned home. She didn't like to see Tío Juan. Seeing Tío Juan made her miss Tía Rosa even more.

One day Carmela said to her mother, "Tía Rosa died before I could give her anything, Mamá. She baked me cookies and taught me to knit and brought me surprises. I was going to surprise her. Now it's too late."

"Carmela, Tía Rosa didn't want her kindness returned. She wanted it passed on," said her mother. "That way a part of Tía Rosa will never die."

"But I wanted to give something to her!" shouted Carmela. "Just to Tía Rosa. To show her that I loved her!"

"She knew that, Carmela. Every smile and hug and visit told her that you loved her," said her mother. "Now it's Tío Juan who needs our love."

"I know," answered Carmela in a soft voice, "but it's hard, Mamá. It hurts so much without Tía Rosa."

One night Carmela's mother asked Tío Juan to dinner. Carmela met him at the door. This time Carmela did not turn away when she saw his sad eyes. Instead, she hugged him tightly.

For the first time in a week, Tío Juan smiled. "Carmelita, tomorrow you must come next door. I would like you to meet my new granddaughter. Her parents have named her Rosita, little Rose, after her grandmother."

Carmela looked down at her silver rose necklace so Tío Juan would not see the tears in her eyes. Tía Rosa knew the baby would be a girl. Then Carmela remembered the unfinished blanket. "Now I know what I can give!" she said.

After dinner Tío Juan went back to the white house. A few minutes later he returned with Tía Rosa's big knitting bag. Very carefully Carmela pulled out the half-finished blanket and wound the soft pink yarn around the needle.

"Around, over, through, and pull. Around, over, through, and pull." Carmela smiled. At last she had a gift for Tía Rosa.

ABOUT THE AUTHOR

A Gift for Tía Rosa was **Karen T. Taha**'s first book. Since then, she has written two others. Mrs. Taha has lived in America, Spain, Mexico, Egypt, and Kuwait. Her favorite part of traveling and living in other countries is getting to know the people in different places. Mrs. Taha has worked as a Spanish teacher in America, an English teacher in Spain and Egypt, and a school library media specialist, but she says that her favorite job is writing children's books.

METAPHOR

Eve
Merriam

Morning is
a new sheet of paper
for you to write on.

Whatever you want to say,
all day,
until night
folds it up
and files it away.

The bright words and the dark words
are gone
until dawn
and a new day
to write on.

Studying the Selection

FIRST IMPRESSIONS
Do you have some special skill that you learned from an older person?

QUICK REVIEW

1. Where had Tía Rosa been for two weeks?
2. How did Carmela feel when she hugged Tía Rosa?
3. Why did Tía Rosa give a silver rose on a chain to Carmela?
4. What was Carmela's first reaction to the news that Tía Rosa had died?

FOCUS

5. What advice did Carmela's mother give her when she said it wasn't too late to give something back to Tía Rosa?
6. Carmela follows her mother's advice at least twice in the story. What are two examples?

CREATING AND WRITING

7. Imagine that you are Carmela and you are bringing a gift for the new baby. It is a pink blanket! You have also made a card for the new baby and her mother. Write a paragraph for the inside of your card that tells how much you loved and appreciated Tía Rosa.

8. Now that you have the message prepared for your card, design a card for a new baby girl. Draw a picture on the front and write a message like "Congratulations on your new baby girl!" Inside the card, copy the little letter you wrote for question #7, and sign your name.

Lesson in Literature ...
GOOD NEIGHBORS

WHAT IS STATED THEME?

- A story's main idea is its **theme**.
- Identifying the main idea is not always easy; sometimes the reader has to work at figuring out what the author's message is.
- When a story's main idea is clearly expressed somewhere in the story, it is called a **stated theme**.
- The stated theme may be found at the beginning, middle, or end of the story.

THINK ABOUT IT!

1. What angered the father each morning?
2. What did the teenagers do to encourage people to keep the neighborhood clean?
3. Read the last line of the story. In your own words, identify the theme of the story.

It was 6 o'clock in the morning. On the second floor, Tasha was asleep in the bedroom she shared with her sister, Tanya. It was October and there was a chill in the air, but both girls liked to sleep with the window open.

Through the mist of sleep and dreams, Tasha could hear her father yelling as he walked to the curb to pick up the newspaper. "Who makes this mess in our neighborhood?" She heard the front door slam shut and fell back asleep.

As Tasha walked to school that morning with Tanya and her friend, Sonia, she talked about all the trash that was on their lawn and the neighbors' lawns. "You know, our block is a really nice block with lots of good families. Who is spoiling it for everyone?"

"It's a little scary to get involved in other people's business, but maybe it's time to find out," Sonia said.

Nearly all of the people who lived on Taylor Road had trash cans with lids. They didn't litter, either. They were busy with jobs and school and mowing their lawns. Many of them had gardens. If they came outside and found a trash can knocked over by raccoons, they just cleaned up the mess. Tasha and Tanya's mom would say, "Hey, the raccoons were here first. You've got to give them some leeway!"

On the way home from school, Tasha said to Sonia, "I've got a good idea. When we get done with our homework, let's start canvassing the neighborhood. If our moms say it's okay, let's start at the first house on the north side of the street. We go down the street on that side and then come back up the other side. We ring the doorbells and ask people what they think of the situation."

Sonia added, "We can also look at which houses might be the source of the problem. Let's bring pads and pencils or pens."

The girls asked their moms what they thought of the idea. Tasha's mom said to be very polite, and to bring a third friend. "How about asking Jennifer?"

Sonia's mom said, "Also ask people if they want to get involved in a neighborhood cleanup."

The girls called Jennifer. She was excited about the project.

They met at 5:00 in front of the first house. They were a little nervous about talking to people they didn't know. Also, it was almost dinnertime. Maybe people would be irritated by the interruption. Should they ring the doorbells of houses that were the source of the trash flying about the neighborhood?

It took a week to talk to people in each house. By that time, they had a Clean Neighborhood campaign going. Other kids their age asked to join. By the following week, there were eight teenagers who were serious about talking to people on the block. They worked in groups of three or four and kept good notes.

Two weeks after Tasha's dad had come in shouting, they made signs about Being Good Neighbors. They taped them to every streetlamp. They picked a Sunday for the cleanup. The team bought large plastic bags. They left the bags posted on the front doorknobs of each house. In each bag was a copy of the notice about having a clean street.

When Sunday arrived, more than fifty Taylor Road residents appeared, bags in hand. The eight teenagers had identified four houses that had trash all over their lawns and porches. One person appeared from one of those houses. The woman looked tired. "I'm sorry. I can't blame my kids, because my husband and I have never talked to the kids about it."

"It's never too late!" Sonia said to the woman. They worked for three hours. It really didn't take very long. Tasha said, "Who would believe that we could do this? I never knew who most of our neighbors were. Before, lots of us were angry. Now, we've seen how people can come together to do something good!"

Blueprint for Reading

INTO . . . *Harlequin and the Gift of Many Colors*

Have you ever seen a patchwork quilt? It is made of small pieces of different fabrics. If you were to place those small pieces next to each other, you wouldn't see how they could possibly match. But somehow, when the pieces are trimmed and sewn together, a beautiful quilt is the result. In this story you will see how a group of friends help someone they all care about. Each gives a small piece of something they own, very much like the parts of a patchwork quilt.

As you read *Harlequin and the Gift of Many Colors*, you will meet a boy who is very poor, unlike his friends. As the story opens, he is shivering in the cold. You will see, though, how very warm his life turns out to be.

EYES ON *Stated Theme*

Do you have an idea that you think about often? You may have shared it with your parents or friends. You may have even written about it in your diary or used it as a topic for a writing assignment. Authors are likely to have certain ideas that they want to share with their readers. Sometimes, when they want to make sure they have gotten their message across, they say it clearly in their stories. When a story's main idea is expressed very clearly, the story has a **stated theme**.

How do you find the stated theme? You start out by reading carefully. In your mind, summarize the personality of the main character, what the other characters say, and the story's plot. As you read *Harlequin and the Gift of Many Colors*, see if you can find one or more places where the author expresses the main idea in a few words. That will be the stated theme.

HARLEQUIN
AND THE GIFT OF
MANY COLORS

ADAPTED FROM A STORY BY
Remy Charlip and Burton Supree

PAINTINGS BY
Remy Charlip

Harlequin[1] awoke. His room was dark. The stars and the moon were still in the sky. It was chilly when he got out of bed, so Harlequin wrapped his blanket around him. When he walked to the window, he felt as if he were wearing the night.

In the dim light, he saw people passing in the street below. They had all left home in the dark to get to the town square early this morning. They were bringing great trays of cakes, pies, and cookies that would be sold tonight. The children were all up helping, too.

But Harlequin sighed. He got back into his warm bed. He pulled the covers over his head.

---

1. *Harlequin* (HAR le KIN) was a comic character who always wore a mask and a colorful, diamond-patterned costume. He often held a sword or a wand in his hand.

The children could hardly wait for tonight's great Carnival. There would be games with prizes and candy and ice cream. And there would be dancing and singing and joking with all their friends.

"But where is Harlequin?" one of the children asked, "I haven't seen him all morning."

Harlequin was almost always the first one up, and the one to lead the others in all sorts of fun.

"Maybe he was bad and his mother won't let him come out."

"Maybe he's sick. We'd better go see." And they all ran off to Harlequin's house.

"Harlequin! Harlequin, are you there?" He appeared at the window wearing his blanket.

"Are you all right? Come on out!" His friends all started talking at once.

"Harlequin, the fireworks are all finished."

"My father says I can stay up as late as I want."

"Can you smell the chocolate?"

"Hurry, let's get back to the square."

Slowly Harlequin dressed and came down.

Walking back to the square, the children began to talk about the best thing of all. Tonight everyone was going to wear a new costume for the first time. With masks over their faces no one would know them. Oh, what tricks they would get away with then!

But it was hard not to brag and tease with little hints about their costumes.

"Mine is yellow."

"My suit is soft and blue."

"Wait till you see mine. It's the most beautiful red."

"I've got the biggest green buttons you ever saw." They were all talking at once, parading around in their old clothes, and showing off as if they were already wearing their new ones.

It was only then that they noticed how quiet and gloomy Harlequin had been all this time.

"What are you going to wear tonight, Harlequin?" They all turned to him.

Harlequin didn't say anything.

"Oh, Harlequin, you've got to tell. We told you."

"Well," said Harlequin, thinking fast, "I'll wear my blanket as a cape."

They thought Harlequin was fooling them as he often did.

"Not that old thing!"

"Come on, Harlequin, give us a clue!"

"What color is it?"

"What are you going to wear tonight?"

"Nothing," Harlequin answered. "I'm not even coming tonight." And he turned and ran away.

Harlequin not coming? How could that be? How could he miss Carnival?

Perhaps he was still fooling. He was always playing tricks.

"Wait," one of them said, "I think I know why he's not coming tonight. He doesn't have a new costume."

And it was then that they all understood what was the matter. Harlequin had nothing to wear because his mother was too poor to buy him a costume.

"What can we do? Where can we get him a costume?" they said.

"I know! I have an idea. My coat doesn't need to be so long. I can cut some off and give it to Harlequin. And if we each give him a piece of cloth, then he will have enough for a whole new costume."

"That's true! My dress doesn't need to be so long either."

"Let's go and get our cloth and meet in front of Harlequin's house."

The sun was high when all the children met at Harlequin's house. Each one was carrying a piece of cloth.

When Harlequin answered the knock on the door, he was surprised to see all his friends. Then they held out the pieces of cloth and happily pushed them into his hands.

But when the children saw Harlequin's arms filled with the cut-off bits and scraps, they were sad. Each piece was a different shape and size and color. Some were shiny, some were fuzzy. None of the pieces matched. They looked like a bunch of old rags.

Harlequin smiled and thanked them. But the children were afraid they had made him more unhappy by giving him such a useless gift.

"I feel so stupid," one of them whispered.

Unhappily they said good-by and left.

When they were gone, Harlequin stared at the scraps of cloth in his arms.

"What can I do with these?" he thought. "Nothing. Not one piece is big enough for a pant leg or even a sleeve."

He climbed the stairs to his room, thinking that he would not go out again until Carnival was over.

He threw the pieces of cloth into the air. But as the pieces fell to the floor, one piece stuck to his shirt. He looked at it for a moment. And then he had an idea.

When his mother came home, Harlequin told her all that had happened.

Then he told her his idea.

"Do you think if we put all these scraps onto my old suit, it would make a good costume?"

His mother looked at the pieces of cloth. She turned them over and over in her hands. Would it work?

Then she smiled, "I think it would be beautiful."

And they both set to work. Harlequin chose a blue piece. Then he pinned a green one next to it. He pinned all the pieces where he wanted them. His mother began to sew them on.

The sewing took a long time. While his mother was sewing the pieces on his old pants, Harlequin climbed into bed to keep warm. And before he knew it, he had fallen asleep.

But his mother worked on, worried that she might not be able to finish in time.

"Wake up, Harlequin, it's all finished!"

Moonlight streamed into his room. He heard music and shouting far away. He blinked his eyes. For a moment he didn't know where he was.

Then he knew he was not dreaming. His mother was standing by his bed, smiling. She was holding up a beautiful rainbow-colored suit.

"It's finished!" He threw the covers off and jumped out of bed. "Let me put it on!"

"How wonderful you look!" his mother said proudly. He spun around and around, as bright as a butterfly. "Oh, thank you, I love it," Harlequin said as he put on his mask and his big hat. "It's wonderful!"

And in a moment he ran off to the town square.

The town square was wild with color and noise. All the world seemed to be dancing and singing there. Wonderful smells of cooking meats and sweet pies filled the air. Musicians were playing all the songs everyone liked to hear.

Harlequin's friends had all come early because the first one to come to a booth to buy something did not have to pay. They laughed and joked as they ran from one booth to another, trying to guess who was behind each mask. But they kept looking out for

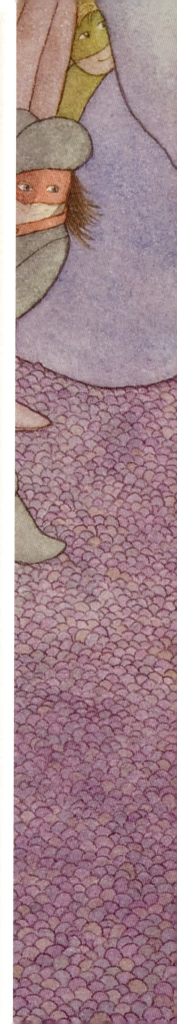

Harlequin, too. They were hoping that by some chance their best friend might be able to come to Carnival.

Suddenly someone appeared in a costume so fantastic that everyone stopped what they were doing. The children all gathered around to see.

"What a splendid costume!"

"I've never seen anything so beautiful!"

"Who is it?"

"Where is he from?"

"Do you know him?" No one knew.

Whoever it was, he began to leap and dance and turn so joyfully that the crowd laughed and clapped with joy. All the many different colors he wore sparkled in the light.

In a flash one of the children noticed a piece of his own costume.

"That piece of blue is mine!" he shouted.

"That shiny red piece is mine!" said another. "That must be Harlequin!"

"Harlequin! Harlequin!" the children cheered, as they raced through the crowd. They danced around, hugging him and each other.

And Harlequin was the happiest of them all on this happy night, for he was clothed in the love of his friends.

ABOUT THE AUTHORS

Remy Charlip and **Burton Supree** coauthored two children's books. In addition to writing books, Mr. Charlip illustrated them, too. To write *Harlequin and the Gift of Many Colors*, Mr. Charlip and Mr. Supree traveled to Italy to do research. The book took them two years to create, since both the writing and the illustrating turned out harder than they expected. Mr. Charlip said, "I had no idea when I started that the book would take so long."

Some people talk and talk
and never say a thing.
Some people look at you
and birds begin to sing.

Some people laugh and laugh
and yet you want to cry.
Some people touch our hand
and music fills the sky.

P
E
O
P
L
E

Charlotte Zolotow

Studying the Selection

QUICK REVIEW

1. Why were the townspeople up and about so early?
2. Why wouldn't Harlequin be able to go to Carnival?
3. What plan did the children have to help Harlequin get a costume?
4. How did the children realize that it was Harlequin inside the costume?

FOCUS

5. The friends wanted to help Harlequin out. They could have each contributed some money for a costume or perhaps loaned him an old costume. Why did the children decide that each of them would give Harlequin a piece of his or her own costume?
6. What is the story's theme?

CREATING AND WRITING

7. What makes someone a real friend? Take out a sheet of paper and write that question at the top. Then, write a list of three qualities that make someone a good friend.
8. Your teacher will distribute scissors, construction paper, and markers to each student. Cut around the edges of your paper so that it looks like a piece of fabric that could be used in a patchwork quilt. Then, draw something on your piece of paper that describes you in some way. Sign your name somewhere on the paper. Your teacher will collect everyone's "patches" and glue them onto a big poster board, forming a "class quilt." One or two of the students will color in the blank spaces between the patches and perhaps glue a border of colored cardboard around the poster board.

A New Girl in Town

WHAT IS IMPLIED THEME?

- To *imply* means to hint at something.
- An **implied theme** is a theme that the author hints at but does not state clearly.
- To discover the implied theme, the reader must identify the one idea that runs through the story.
- To identify that idea, the reader must ask questions, make comparisons, and look for clues. In short, the reader must be a good detective.

THINK ABOUT IT!

1. Why did Karen dread the first day in a new school?
2. What did Karen learn about herself when she helped Brenda with her homework?
3. Think about Karen and how she changed in the story. What is the story's implied theme?

Karen's family had just moved to Greenwood. First her father, and then her mother, had found good jobs there. Greenwood was supposed to be a super place to live—pretty houses, lots of trees, big yards, and excellent schools. But Karen hated moving to a new place. She was very shy and she had a limp. Now she would have to start all over again and make new friends.

The first day of school was worse than she expected. Her teachers were friendly and helpful, but several of her classmates avoided walking home with her. She knew they thought of her as "different."

Her mom and dad told her it would get better over time—it was always difficult in the beginning, coming to live in a new place. Still, the next day she took a different, longer route to school. She avoided the classmates who lived near her, but it took a lot more time to get to school. At the end of the day, she went the same long way to get home.

Several days passed, with Karen taking a different route each day. The second week of school, a girl in her class came over to her during recess. She said her name was Brenda, and asked if Karen would like to walk home with her.

Karen hesitated. "You know it will take longer if you walk with me."

Brenda said, "My dad's got a limp so that's no big deal. Besides, it will give us more time to talk." At first, Karen was delighted. Then she worried that Brenda had offered because she felt bad for her.

They walked together every day after that. Brenda lived farther from the school, so they always parted at Karen's house. They seemed to have a lot in common. They each had a dog. They both had a much younger sister and brother. They both liked to play chess.

The day came when Brenda had an accident and broke her arm. Her doctor said she should remain at home for several days. When Brenda phoned Karen to tell her what had happened, Karen wondered what it would be like to walk alone again. Then she reminded herself that it was Brenda about whom she should be concerned.

The next morning, on the way to school, Karen dropped off some muffins she had made for Brenda. "Wow!" Brenda exclaimed. "Thanks! I'll have these for breakfast."

Once more, Karen took the back route to school. *Well, I may be a good baker*, Karen thought to herself, *but I'm still a coward.*

That afternoon, she brought Brenda her homework. They sat at the desk in Brenda's room, and Karen went over the work with her friend. Brenda said, "Do you know how to do this math?" Karen took the pencil and showed Brenda how to do each of the word problems.

Brenda sighed. "You are so good at this. I bet you could be elected class treasurer." Karen just laughed.

Later, though, when Karen was back home, she thought about what Brenda had said. *I am good at math, and I am a good friend!*

Then she saw the other kids walking towards her. *I have nothing to be afraid of,* she thought. "Hi!" she shouted to them. "It's nice to see you. Brenda's doing really well." Karen smiled. She had had to force the words out of her mouth. But she had said them. Then she continued home.

Blueprint for Reading

INTO . . . *Claw Foot*

What makes a great leader? Is it courage? Is it wisdom? Is it strength? All of those qualities are important in a leader, but, alone, they are not enough. The one quality leaders *must* have is putting the needs of the people they are leading before their own. Even if their own problems are great, even if they will lose out by helping their people, they will put the people first. In *Claw Foot*, two strong people meet each other. One is a leader, and the other is a future leader. Each has a problem with which he lives. But each one has learned to put his people first. As you read *Claw Foot*, watch a young Sioux Indian develop from a boy who is completely absorbed in his own problem, into a leader, whose needy people become his only concern.

EYES ON *Implied Theme*

Are you a good detective? When you read a story, you sometimes have to do a little detective work to uncover the theme. You have to read the story, think about the plot and the characters, review in your mind what the narrator has said, and decide what the main idea of the story is. Sometimes, the author makes it easy for you and states the theme somewhere in the story or poem—all you have to do is spot it! Most of the time, though, the author wants you to work at uncovering the message. When the theme is not obvious and the reader has to "put two and two together," we say that the story has an **implied theme**. As you read *Claw Foot*, consider the plot and the two main characters. What do they have in common? With a little thought, you will uncover the story's implied theme.

An excerpt from

Claw Foot

Evelyn Witter

A young Sioux[1] boy looked down at his gnarled, twisted foot. "The only son of a great Sioux chief should be strong and swift," thought Claw Foot bitterly. "Why was I, of all people, born with such a foot?"

As Claw Foot grew, he learned to deal with the taunts of some of the boys. He tried to remember the advice Big Owl, his father's friend, had given him. "You cannot change your foot. But you cannot let one foot be more important than the

1. The *Sioux* (SOO) were a tribe of Indians who lived along the Missouri and Mississippi Rivers.

rest of your body. You must use what you have and not feel sorry for what you have not." Claw Foot made a decision. He would do so many wonderful deeds that his name would be changed. He would not be called "Claw Foot" forever; he would earn a new and better name.

The first great deed Claw Foot did was to heal the leg of a wounded, wild horse. The horse, Shadow, became the young boy's feet. On Shadow, Claw Foot could fly like the wind. Claw Foot decided he could not wait until he reached manhood to do great deeds. When he learned that the tribe was starving, he set out on Shadow to search for buffalo. Two other young Indians followed him secretly. Just after they discovered buffalo, some Crow Indians discovered all three of the boys on their land. The Crow, enemies of the Sioux, put ropes around the three Sioux boys and brought them to their chief.

In front of a tepee decorated with many paintings, the Crow braves made a sign for their captives to dismount. Claw Foot slid from his horse's back. He saw firelight behind the flap of the tepee and smelled the strong odor of food.

His captor pushed him into the tepee. White Feather and Red Duck stumbled in beside him. The chief of the Crow sat cross-legged on a robe not far from the fire. He had broad shoulders. His face looked as if it were carved from the rock of the ridges that surrounded the village. The Crow with the two eagle feathers spoke, but Claw Foot did not understand his language.

> ### WORD BANK
>
> **captives** (KAP tivs)
> *n.*: people that are captured
>
> **dismount** (DIS mount)
> *v.*: to get off a horse

The chief looked from one to the other. There was a grim, set look on his face. He looked hard and straight into Claw Foot's eyes.

Claw Foot tried to stand straight. He knew that the Crow, like the Sioux, hated a show of weakness. There was a long silence. The chief studied Claw Foot's gnarled foot, which even Falling Star's carefully made moccasin could not disguise. As the chief stared, his right hand went awkwardly to his left arm. Claw Foot saw that the chief's left arm was twisted and bent to uselessness.

The chief spoke. He addressed himself to Claw Foot. "I know your language," he said. "What are you called?"

"I am Claw Foot," Claw Foot answered, even though he hated saying his name.

"I am Broken Wing," the chief said. "It was not always so. On a buffalo hunt many moons ago ..." The chief did not finish. His eyes were sad.

"Why do you come to the land of the Crow?" Broken Wing asked.

Claw Foot still felt afraid. But he knew this was his chance to save himself and the others. If he could stir the sympathy that he sensed behind that rigid face, perhaps the Crow would not harm them.

WORD BANK

gnarled (NARLD) *adj.*: bent and twisted

disguise (dis GIZE) *v.*: to hide the way something looks

awkwardly (AWK wurd lee) *adv.*: uneasily; uncomfortably

uselessness (YOOS less ness) *n.*: not serving any purpose; of no use

addressed (uh DRESSD) *v.*: directed his words to

sympathy (SIM puh thee) *n.*: the ability to share the sorrow of another person

rigid (RIH jid) *adj.*: stiff and motionless

Claw Foot swallowed hard. Then he spoke. "My people are near starvation. Our herds are gone. Our braves have traveled many moons to find buffalo," Claw Foot told the chief.

"You were brave but foolish to come to our land," Broken Wing said.

"I want to help my people!" Claw Foot cried. "My foot, my name … they are not important. My people may die!" He straightened his tired shoulders.

Broken Wing's eyes looked into his. A light flickered in them for an instant. Claw Foot felt a surge of hope. Broken Wing understood!

Claw Foot waited anxiously for Broken Wing's next words. Behind him, Red Duck's breathing was loud. He heard White Feather catch his breath between his teeth.

Broken Wing finally spoke. "You put the need of your people above your own. My people, too, are more important than this useless arm," he said. "Claw Foot, I shall give you one buffalo that my hunters have killed. I shall let you and your friends go back to your people. But I will have your word that you will not come to Crow land again."

"But one buffalo will not last long." Claw Foot could not keep the pleading tone from his voice.

"One buffalo. Meat and hide," said Broken Wing. "Take your buffalo when the sun rises. Be thankful that the Crow did not kill you."

WORD BANK

pleading (PLEED ing)
n.: begging

Suddenly, as Claw Foot thought about the uselessness of one buffalo for the many moons ahead, an idea came to him. It made his heart beat fast. He would try once more for his people.

"May I have the land that this one buffalo hide will cover?" he asked.

Broken Wing scowled. "That is a foolish request," he said. "One hide would not cover enough ground for one tepee."

"Perhaps I can stretch the hide," Claw Foot said.

Broken Wing frowned. He looked at Claw Foot's moccasin. Then his eyes studied Claw Foot's face with a look Claw Foot had seen before. He had seen it on his father's face many times. It was a look that said, "He is young and foolish, but he tries, and tries, and tries."

"You may have the land one hide covers," Broken Wing nodded.

"And I must have the freedom to ride over your land to find a place for my hide," Claw Foot said with new confidence.

> ### WORD BANK
>
> **confidence** (KAHN fih DENTS) *n.*: belief in oneself

At Broken Wing's hesitation, he added, "I will not try to escape. We will not do anything wrong. I give my word as a Sioux."

Broken Wing nodded. The three captives were untied and led away by the brave with two eagle feathers. Claw Foot was pushed roughly into a tepee at the far side of the circle. A stewpot hung over a fire, and there were robes on which to sleep.

"What can we do with the land one hide covers?" scoffed Red Duck between gulps of food.

White Feather stopped eating, a strip of buffalo meat dripping in his fingers, and waited for Claw Foot's answer.

But Claw Foot did not want to disturb his thoughts by answering Red Duck. He needed to lay his plans carefully. He dipped into the buffalo stew and did not answer. His wrists were bruised and sore, but he gave them little thought. He thought of his plan.

> ### WORD BANK
>
> **hesitation** (HEZ ih TAY shun) *n.*: a delay due to uncertainty or fear
>
> **bruised** (BROOZED) *adj.*: slightly injured

His plan was clear when the sun came up over the edge of the world. He knew what he had to do. He found the part of the camp where the buffalo was skinned and the meat cut up in chunks. There he picked up the buffalo that Broken Wing had promised him. Claw Foot dragged the hide to the grassy spot where his horse, Shadow, was tied. He threw the hide over the gray horse's shoulder and climbed on.

Shadow tossed his head and stamped a front hoof. Claw Foot dug his heels into Shadow's flanks and turned the horse's head to the south. Then, in a flash of movement, Shadow broke from a trot to a gallop.

Claw Foot rode beyond the ridges, far to the south. Only occasionally he stopped to gulp clear water from a stream and to rest Shadow. He saw signs of buffalo, and his heart sang.

Then, as Shadow trotted at an easy pace, Claw Foot
drew out his knife, which was still hidden in his belt.
He began cutting pieces of hide and throwing them on
the ground.

He cut piece after piece, scattering them great
distances apart. When he no longer had a single scrap
of hide left, he turned Shadow toward the Crow village.

There was an orange sun going down over the edge of the world when Claw Foot approached the village. His heart beat fast at the thought that he would soon be facing Broken Wing again. Would Broken Wing keep his word?

Back at Broken Wing's tepee, he lifted the flap and entered. There, right before him, stood Big Owl, a brave Sioux warrior! The Crow with the two eagle feathers stood to one side. Broken Wing sat crossed-legged before the fire. He stopped talking when he saw Claw Foot.

"Big Owl!" Claw Foot cried.

There was a hint of reproach in Big Owl's eyes. "I am glad I found you," he said.

"Found me?" Claw Foot asked.

"When I returned to our village after scouting for buffalo and you were gone—you and White Feather and Red Duck—Hurries-to-War agreed that I must find you," Big Owl explained. With that, his captor pushed him and made a sign for him to be quiet.

"The Crow found me first," Big Owl added, ignoring the brave with two eagle feathers.

Claw Foot took another step forward. He talked to the chief. "Big Owl is my friend. You promised to let my friends go."

The chief hesitated. "Broken Wing keeps a promise," he finally said.

Claw Foot was relieved. Broken Wing's words gave him the courage to ask the question upon which so much depended.

He swallowed hard against a lump in his throat and said, "I have come for my land."

"What land?" asked Broken Wing.

"The land one buffalo hide covers," Claw Foot answered.

Broken Wing was thoughtful. "My scouts tell me you cut the buffalo hide in many pieces and threw the pieces on the ground."

"The pieces are spread over enough land for my people. Enough land to make a village and hunt the buffalo," Claw Foot explained.

Big Owl shot him a quick glance of admiration.

Broken Wing looked up at Claw Foot and then at his moccasined feet. He said, "Only your body is lame, not your thoughts. You have outwitted me fairly. You may have the land."

WORD BANK

admiration (AD mih RAY shun) *n.*: respect and approval

outwitted (out WIT ed) *v.*: outsmarted

Claw Foot thanked Broken Wing solemnly, hoping his voice did not show how much relief he felt. He looked up at Big Owl. But the warrior's head was bent in deep thought.

At last Big Owl raised his eyes and spoke to Claw Foot. "From this day on," he said, "you will not be known as Claw Foot. From this day on your name is He Who Thinks."

Claw Foot thought his chest would burst from holding back shouts of joy!

WORD BANK

solemnly (SOLL uhm lee)
adv.: seriously

As he and Big Owl left the tepee, Claw Foot looked happily at the other two captives, who were standing just outside. He looked from one face to the other.

White Feather had a look of bewildered pleasure as he shouted, "Hoye!"[2]

Red Duck turned toward Claw Foot and hung his head to avoid Claw Foot's eyes.

"He Who Thinks, you are a leader among our people," he said. "One day you will be chief. I hope that I may be among your warriors."

"I am thankful for my new name," said He Who Thinks. "I shall try to keep it a strong name for the good of my people."

---

2. *Hoye* (ha OH) is an expression of enthusiastic agreement.

He turned and whistled to Shadow. And as he mounted the proud gray horse, he was silently thankful for his good fortune. By serving his people, he had at last earned for himself a name befitting the son of a great chief. He Who Thinks knew that this was truly the most important day of his life.

WORD BANK

befitting (bih FIT ing) *adj.*: proper for; fitting

Beauty

E-YEH-SHURE´

Beauty is seen
In the sunlight,
The trees, the birds,
Corn growing and people working
Or dancing for their harvest.

Beauty is heard
In the night,
Wind sighing, rain falling,
Or a singer chanting
Anything in earnest.

Beauty is in yourself.
Good deeds, happy thoughts
That repeat themselves
In your dreams,
In your work,
And even in your rest.

Studying the Selection

FIRST IMPRESSIONS

Have you ever been called a name that embarrassed you? What did you do about it?

QUICK REVIEW

1. What tribe did Claw Foot belong to?

2. Why was Claw Foot given that name?

3. What did Broken Wing offer to give Claw Foot for his people?

4. What additional request did Claw Foot make?

FOCUS

5. In what positive way did Claw Foot deal with his hurtful name?

6. Compare Broken Wing to Claw Foot in the following two ways:

   a. How were they similar physically?

   b. What did both of them consider more important than anything else?

CREATING AND WRITING

7. Imagine that once the Crow Indians allowed the Sioux Indians to live on their land, the two tribes decided to make a peace treaty. Take a piece of scratch paper and write down four rules that both tribes would need to obey in order to keep the peace. Then, on construction paper or poster board, design a peace treaty document. Draw an appropriate border, print out the words Peace Treaty between the Sioux and Crow Nations, and write out the four rules. At the bottom, sign the names of the two chiefs, or draw a picture of their names. For the Crow chief, use the name Broken Wing. For the Sioux chief, make up a name.

8. What is the name of your street? Give it an "Indian" name that describes it in some way. For example, you could name it "Street of Many Trees," or "Lilac Bush Lane." Your teacher will give you materials to make a street sign. Print out the new name of your street and draw a picture to illustrate it.

Lesson in Literature ...
THE FRESH AIR FUND

DRAWING CONCLUSIONS

- **Drawing conclusions** means using the information we have to predict what will happen in the story.
- As we read, we notice details and clues about how the story will turn out.
- We begin to "put two and two together" to figure out what will happen.
- At the end of the story, we see whether our conclusions were correct. In a mystery, or a story with a surprise ending, they may not have been!

THINK ABOUT IT!

1. Why do the children in the story need to get away from New York in the summer?
2. How is life at camp different from life in the city? List at least three differences.
3. From reading about Myah, Faye, and Derrick, what conclusions could you draw about what Fresh Air camps accomplish?

New York City is a very hot, muggy place in the summertime. For many children, there is not a lot to do each day when there is no school. This is especially true in the poorer sections of the city, where some kids may get into trouble. That's when it's the Fresh Air Fund to the rescue!

FRESH AIR FACTS:

- People donate money to Fresh Air to pay for Fresh Air programs.
- For Fresh Air, families open their homes to children. These families provide a "home away from home" that is not in the hot city.
- Fresh Air has five camps on 2,300 acres in the country. Fresh Air has given free camp summers to more than 1.7 million children from poor communities.
- At Fresh Air camps, no electronics of any kind are allowed. Fresh Air shows kids life is more than staying home, playing video games, and hanging out on the street.
- Fresh Air has year-round educational programs.
- Many children go to Fresh Air weekend camps all year round.
- Fresh Air helps make happy children and good citizens.

FRESH AIR CHILDREN: MYAH, FAYE, AND DERRICK

Myah is nine years old. What does she love about camp? Myah loves swimming, her new friends, and the quiet. Does she swim in a pool? No! The campers swim in a real lake. This is what she says: "I feel very peaceful and I love going to sleep hearing the crickets." Myah had never been away from home for so long, but at camp she has very good friends and counselors. Now she has hiked, roasted marshmallows, and seen deer and lizards. During their free time, Myah and her friends sit out on their cabin porch. "We talk about everything. We understand each other."

This year Faye is a junior counselor at a Fresh Air camp. Her job has forced her to be more mature, to be upbeat and to be caring, even when she doesn't feel like it. This has helped her to be a better person, she says. She says she is happier and much more patient than she was before. She has learned to listen.

When she was younger, she spent four summers as a camper. "This made me more self-confident," Faye says. Faye wants her campers to enjoy camp as much as she did. She also knows that it can be difficult to adjust to camp—forests and fields, complete darkness at night, and animals she had never seen before. What a shock it was! But within just two weeks, she felt at home. "Here, the air is clean and cool. You can smell the grass and the trees. I love it."

When he was just six, Derrick's mom found out about the Fresh Air Fund. He began spending summers with Fresh Air Fund families. At 16, he started training as a counselor. He says that when he was younger, the Fresh Air Fund saved his life.

"It has changed the course of my life, as well. It protected me from the dangers of the city and made me who I am today." Derrick is now a college student, but he comes back to work as a counselor each summer. "The people here are my family. I look forward to coming all year." He has watched with pride as many of his own campers change from "troubled boys to confident young men."

WE ♥ THE FRESH AIR FUND

FRESH AIR FUND CONCLUSION

Every summer, 3,000 kids from some of New York City's toughest neighborhoods go to Fresh Air camps and families. These are kids who have never slept in a cabin, swum in a lake, sat around a campfire, or gone on an overnight hike and slept in tents. At camp, they will make new friends, and experience the freedom of space, calm, and the quiet of nature. The Fresh Air Fund changes the lives of 9,000 New York City children each year.

Blueprint for Reading

INTO . . . *Beatrice's Goat*

Do you ever want something very badly but simply don't have the money to buy it? Your parents might tell you to wait and they will get it for you. Or, they might suggest a way that you can earn the money to buy it for yourself. Which would you prefer?

Beatrice is a young girl from a very poor African family. What she wants most is the chance to go to school. As you read *Beatrice's Goat*, you will see how she finally gets her wish. A group of people who help poor families in Africa make it possible. Did they make it easy for Beatrice to get her wish? The easiest way is not always the best way.

EYES ON *Drawing Conclusions*

Have you ever heard the expression, "to put two and two together"? It means that you have enough information to figure out what *has* happened or *will* happen. For example, your mother walks into the kitchen and sees the baby sitting on the floor covered in jam. The cupboard where the jam is usually locked up is open, and the only one who was in the kitchen earlier is you. Your mother "puts two and two together" and figures out what *has happened*: you are the one who left the cupboard unlocked and the jam jar loosely covered. Next, you walk in and see the baby and your mother's frown; you "put two and two together" and figure out what *will happen*!

The expression **drawing conclusions** means the same thing as "putting two and two together." When we read a story, we look at the information that has been presented, and decide what the story's theme is. Most readers prefer a story that allows them to think for themselves. A good story gives us information but does not openly tell us what to think.

BEATRICE'S GOAT

PAGE McBRIER

IF you were to visit the small African village of Kisinga[1] in the rolling hills of western Uganda,[2] and if you were to take a left at the crossroads and follow a narrow dirt path between two tall banana groves, you would come to the home of a girl named Beatrice.

Beatrice lives here with her mother and five younger brothers and sisters in a sturdy mud house with a fine steel roof. The house is new. So is the shiny blue wooden furniture inside. In fact, many things are new to Beatrice and her family lately.

_____

1. *Kisinga* (kih SING uh)
2. *Uganda* (oo GAN duh)

WORD BANK

sturdy (STUR dee) *adj.:* strong and not easily broken

And it's all because of a goat named Mugisa.[3]

Beatrice loves everything about Mugisa … the feel of her coarse brown-and-white coat, the way her chin hairs curl just so, and how Mugisa gently teases her by butting her knobby horns against Beatrice's hand—*tup*, *tup*—like a drumbeat waiting for a song.

But there is one reason why Beatrice loves Mugisa most of all.

In the time before Mugisa, Beatrice spent her days helping her mama hoe and plant in the fields, tend the chickens, watch the younger children, and grind the cassava flour[4] that they would take to market to sell.

_____

3. *Mugisa* (moo GEE sah)
4. *Cassava flour* is flour made from the roots of the cassava, a tropical American plant.

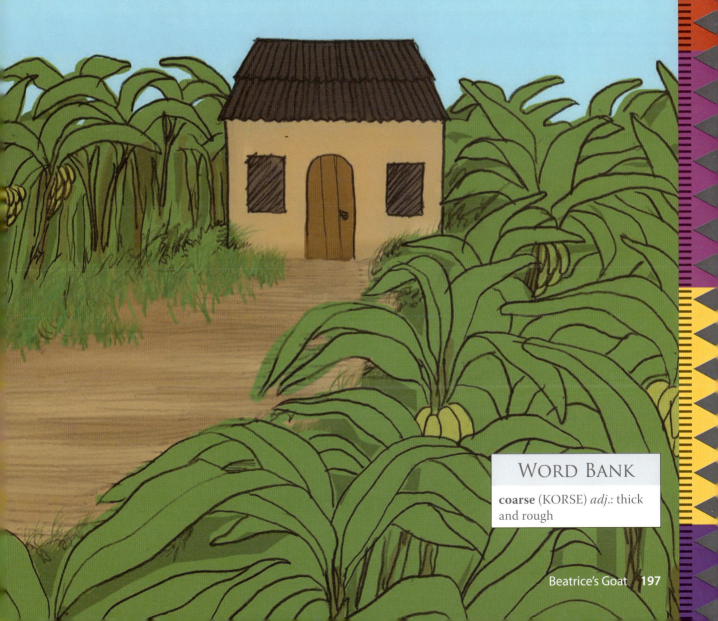

WORD BANK

coarse (KORSE) *adj.*: thick and rough

Once in a while, when she was tending baby Paskavia,[5] Beatrice would stop by the schoolhouse. Often, the students had carried their long wooden benches outside to work under the cool shade of the jackfruit trees. Then Beatrice would stand quietly off to one side, pretending she was a student, too.

Oh, how she longed to be a schoolgirl! How she yearned to sit on one of the benches and figure sums on a small slate chalkboard.[6] How she wished to turn the pages of a worn copybook and study each word over and over until it stuck in her mind like a burr.[7]

"I'll never be able to go to school," she would sigh. "How could I ever save enough money to pay for books or a uniform?"

_____

5. *Paskavia (*pas KAH vee uh) is Beatrice's baby sister.

6. In the past, children would write with chalk on small *slate chalkboards* that they held in their laps or placed on their desks. These were similar to the large chalkboards found on classroom walls.

7. *Burrs* are little, thorny balls. If a burr gets into someone's hair or clothing, or into an animal's fur, it is almost impossible to get them out. When Beatrice hopes the words she learns will *stick in her mind like a burr*, she means she hopes she will never forget them.

WORD BANK

yearned (YURND)
v.: wanted very, very much

One day while Beatrice was busy pulling weeds, Mama came to her with dancing eyes. "Beatrice, some kindhearted people from far away have given us a lucky gift. We are one of twelve village families to receive a goat."

Beatrice was puzzled. A goat? What kind of gift was a goat? It couldn't get up each morning and start their charcoal fire for cooking. It couldn't hike down to the stream each week and scrub their dirty clothes clean. It couldn't keep an eye on Grace, Moses, Harriet, Joash, and Paskavia.

Her long fingers tugged patiently at the weeds. "That's very nice, Mama," she said politely.

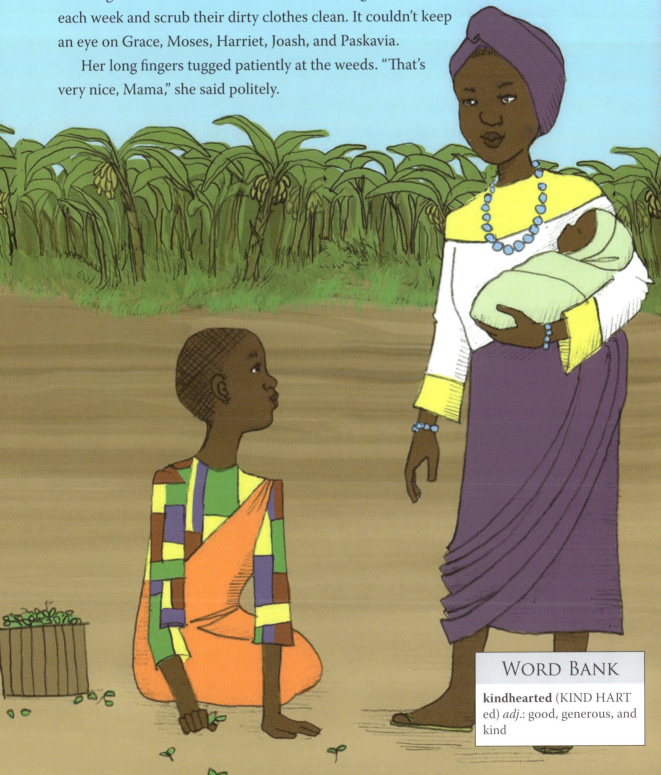

WORD BANK

kindhearted (KIND HART ed) *adj.*: good, generous, and kind

Then Mama added, "It will be your job to take care of our goat. If you do, it can bring wonderful things."

Beatrice looked up at her mother. "Will this goat come soon?" she asked. "Because I would like to meet such a goat."

Mama laughed. "Good things take time. First I must plant pastures and build our goat a shed."

Beatrice nodded slowly. Surely Mama knew what she was doing. "I will help you," she declared.

For the next few months, Beatrice worked harder than ever. She helped Mama collect the posts for the shed walls, then lashed the posts together with banana fibers.[8] She planted narrow bands of stiff elephant grass along the edges of their cassava field. She put in pigeon trees and lab lab vines between the banana trees.

---

8. *Banana fibers* are long, stringy parts of the banana plant that are surprisingly strong. They can be used like twine, as they are in this story, and are sometimes spun into yarn to be used in fabrics.

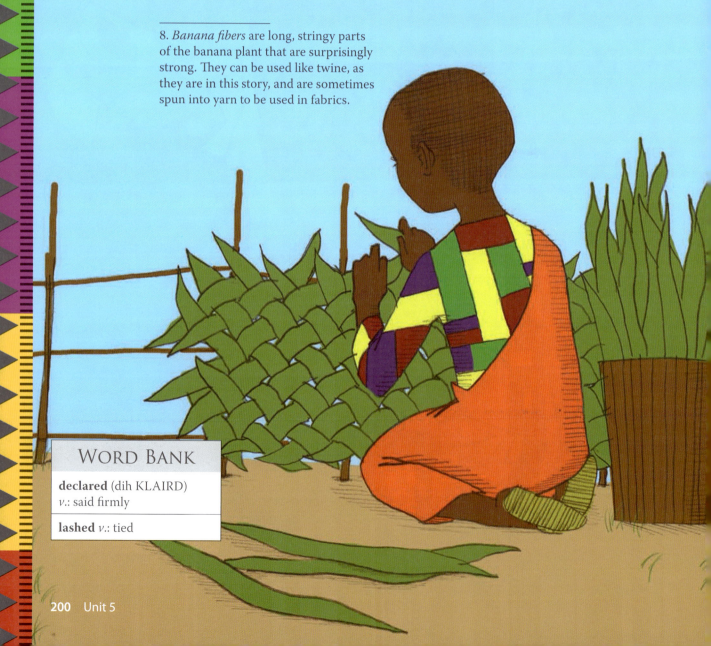

WORD BANK

declared (dih KLAIRD)
v.: said firmly

lashed *v.*: tied

Finally, one day Beatrice's goat arrived, fat and sleek as a ripe mango. Beatrice stood shyly with her brothers and sisters, then stepped forward and circled the goat once. She knelt close, inspecting its round belly, and ran her hand along its smooth back. "Mama says you are our lucky gift," she whispered. "So that is what I will name you. Mugisa ... luck."

Two weeks later, Mugisa gave birth. It was Beatrice who discovered first one kid and then, to her surprise, another. "Twins!" she exclaimed, stooping down to examine them. "See that, my Mugisa? You have already brought us *two* wonderful things." Beatrice named the first kid *Mulindwa*,[9] which means expected, and the second *Kihembo*,[10] or surprise.

Each day Beatrice made sure Mugisa got extra elephant grass and water to help her produce lots of milk, even though it meant another long trip down to the stream and back.

When the kids no longer needed it, Beatrice took her own first taste of Mugisa's milk. "Mmm. Sweet," she said,

_____

9. *Mulindwa* (muh LIND wah)
10. *Kihembo* (kih HEM bo)

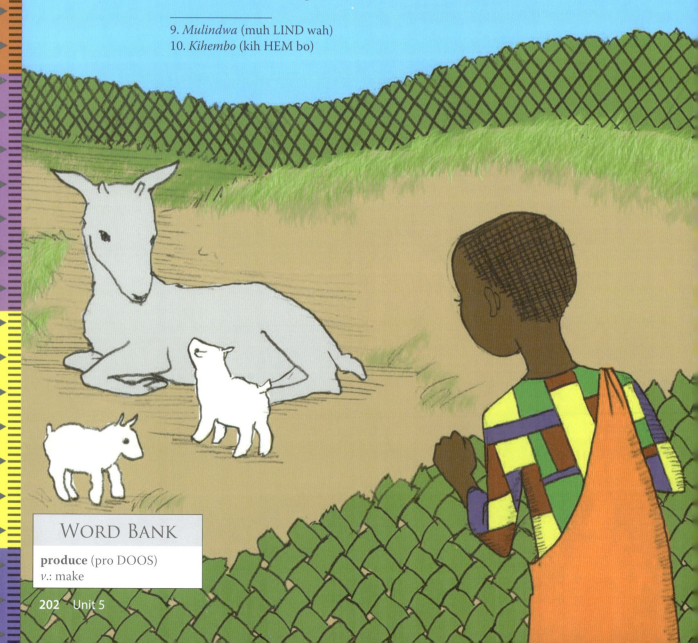

WORD BANK

produce (pro DOOS)
v.: make

mixing the rest into her cup of breakfast porridge. Beatrice knew Mugisa's milk would keep them all much healthier.

Now, each morning after breakfast, Beatrice would head off to the shed to see whatever milk was left over. "Open for business," she would say, in case anyone was listening.

Often she would spy her friend Bunane[11] coming through the banana groves.

"Good morning, Beatrice, Mugisa, Expected, and Surprise," Bunane would always say. Then he would hand Beatrice a tall pail that she would fill to the top with Mugisa's milk.

When Beatrice finished pouring, Bunane would hand her a shiny coin, and Beatrice would carefully tuck the money into the small woven purse at her side.

Day after day, week after week, Beatrice watched the purse get fuller. Soon there would be enough money for a new shirt for Moses and a warm blanket for the bed she shared with Grace.

11. *Bunane* (boo NAH nay)

One day, Beatrice returned from collecting water and noticed Mama frowning and counting the money in her woven purse. Beatrice put down the water can and rushed to her mother's side. "Mama! What is it?" she asked. "What's wrong?"

As she looked up, Mama's frown turned to a small smile. "I think," she said, "you may just have saved enough to pay for school."

"School?" Beatrice gasped in disbelief. "But what about all the other things we need?"

"First things first," Mama said.

Beatrice threw her arms around her mother's neck. "Oh, Mama, thank you." Then she ran to where her goat stood chewing her cud and hugged her tight. "Oh, Mugisa!" she whispered. "Today *I* am the lucky one. You have given me the gift I wanted most."

WORD BANK

disbelief (DIS bih LEEF)
n.: not believing

The very next week Beatrice started school. On the first morning that she was to attend, she sat proudly waiting for milk customers in her new yellow blouse and blue jumper, Mugisa by her side.

Beatrice felt nervous and excited at the same time. Mugisa pressed close, letting her coarse coat brush softly against Beatrice's cheek. "Oh, Mugisa," Beatrice cried. "I'll miss you today!"

Then she thought again about all the good things Mugisa was bringing. Mama said that soon Surprise would be sold for a lot of money. "It will be enough to tear down this old house," she had explained. "We will be able to put up a new one with a steel roof that won't leak during the rains."

Beatrice heard a rustle and noticed Bunane heading toward her with his empty milk pail. He eyed her new uniform and sighed, "You're so lucky. I wish *I* could go to school."

Beatrice reached out and touched Bunane's arm. "I've heard that your family is next in line to receive a goat."

A smile crossed Bunane's face. "Really?"

"Really."

Then Beatrice kissed Mugisa
on the soft part of her nose, close
to where her chin hairs curled just
so, and started off to school.

ABOUT THE AUTHOR

Page McBrier had quite a colorful
childhood. She grew up in a large
family with lots of pets, including
dogs, cats, chickens, ducks, mice,
turtles, an alligator, and a mule,
which she and her siblings would
sometimes ride to school and tie to
the bike rack! Mrs. McBrier always
wanted to work with children.
When writing *Beatrice's Goat*,
which is based on a true story,
Mrs. McBrier traveled to East
Africa to research and to meet the
real Beatrice.

Studying the Selection

QUICK REVIEW

1. What did Beatrice want more than anything in the world?
2. What two things did Mama have to do before Mugisa arrived?
3. How did Beatrice earn money for the family?
4. When Bunane looked sad because he could not go to school, what did Beatrice say to cheer him up?

FOCUS

5. Why do you think Beatrice wanted to go to school?
6. Why do you think the "kindhearted people from far away" gave the family a goat instead of just buying Beatrice books and a uniform?

CREATING AND WRITING

7. Beatrice was a real girl who came to America to go to college. While she was in the United States, she visited many schools to tell other students how Mugisa helped her get what she wanted most—an education! Imagine that you are Beatrice and write a short speech about your life in Uganda, what a great gift Mugisa was, and the importance of education.
8. Using the speech that you wrote for question #7, prepare to present it to your class. Draw at least one picture that you can use as a "photograph" to show the class what life was like in Uganda. Your teacher will allow one or two students to ask you questions about your speech. Be prepared to answer them.

Lesson in Literature ...
LETTERS TO A FRIEND

COMPARE AND CONTRAST

- The ability to *compare and contrast* is an important part of any learning.
- **Comparing** means finding the similarities in two or more things.
- **Contrasting** means finding the differences in two or more things.
- Comparing and contrasting characters, settings, and different parts of the plot help us to identify a story's theme.

THINK ABOUT IT!

1. Read Helen's first letter to Emilia, and contrast the way Helen used to dress with the way she dresses on the trail.

2. Contrast the way the Sioux actually behaved with the way Emilia probably thought of the Sioux.

3. Compare Helen to Mama in at least two ways.

July 2, 1853

Dear Emilia,

As I write, I wonder if you have received my first and second letters. Given how difficult things are on the trail, perhaps the mail has never gotten through.

Do you remember how particular I used to be about my hair and my dresses? And how much we talked about being in fashion? You should see me now! It is hard to stay clean on the trail. We wear our clothes for a really long time without changing them. I guess a person can get accustomed to anything!

I haven't received any letters from you. Did you write back? I miss you so much. Oh, I have to run and go wash dishes!

Your best friend,
Helen

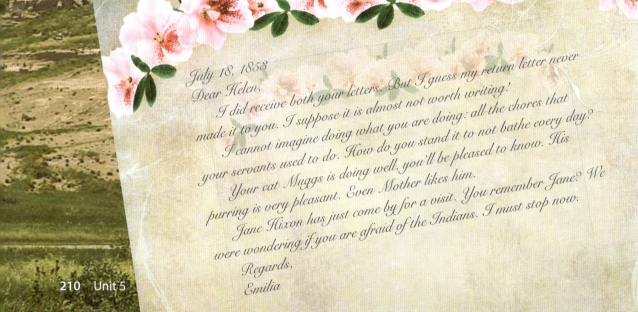

July 18, 1853

Dear Helen,

I did receive both your letters. But I guess my return letter never made it to you. I suppose it is almost not worth writing! I cannot imagine doing what you are doing: all the chores that your servants used to do. How do you stand it to not bathe every day? Your cat Muggs is doing well, you'll be pleased to know. His purring is very pleasant. Even Mother likes him. Jane Hixon has just come by for a visit. You remember Jane? We were wondering if you are afraid of the Indians. I must stop now.

Regards,
Emilia

July 31, 1853
Dear Emilia,

I so much miss the fun and the long talks we used to have. I do hope I hear from you soon. Regarding cleanliness, when we crossed the Platte, we found that it was too shallow and too muddy for washing and bathing. (I still couldn't wait to get into that cool, sandy water. It's been so hot.)

Maybe it was good the Platte is shallow. When we cross a river that's too high, we have to unload everything inside the wagons—Pa says it's about two thousand pounds of stuff—and place it on rafts. Then we have to repack all of it on the other side of the river. That's a ladies' job. Mama and I have gotten really good at it.

Mama has such a positive attitude and she wants Pa to be proud of us. I don't know how she does it with the baby coming. I'm lucky my Mama is so strong and brave. I look up to her so much now.

Friends,
Helen

August 21, 1853
Dear Emilia,

We have been through broad yellow Nebraska and part of Wyoming. The days are hot and the nights cool, but as we got higher up, we had hailstorms with hail the size of snowballs. The only Sioux we met wanted to barter or be hired as guides.

We just reached a place called Fort Hall. It's good to have a rest, especially for Mama.

After we leave Fort Hall, the Oregon and California Trails split in northwesterly and southwesterly directions. Of course, we are taking the Oregon Trail. Would you believe we've traveled twelve hundred miles so far, and we are only halfway to our destination? I worry, because they say the worst is yet to come.

I will let you in on a secret. Mama's baby should come in the next few days!

Hope all is well with you and your family and Muggs. I hope I hear from you sometime.

Friends?
Helen

Blueprint for Reading

INTO . . . *The Gardener*

How do you get people to smile? Well, that all depends on why they are not smiling. Are they in pain? Are they unhappy? Are they angry? If a friend doesn't smile at you, you can always ask what is wrong. If a stranger doesn't smile, you can just forget about it and go about your business. But sometimes, the person is right in the middle—not a friend, yet not a stranger. In *The Gardener*, a girl named Lydia Grace is sent to live with her uncle. He is kind and generous, but never looks happy. It is not easy to spend a lot of time with someone so serious. What can she do to bring a smile to his face? As you read *The Gardener*, watch how Lydia Grace behaves and think about how she works out a way to bring happiness to someone who needs a little sunshine in his life.

EYES ON *Compare and Contrast*

Have you ever gone shopping for shoes? How do you decide which pair to buy? You probably try on a few pairs and *compare and contrast* them. When you **compare** them, you are asking how they are alike. When you **contrast** them, you are asking how they are different. Comparing and contrasting are some of the most useful tools in getting to know anything at all, from characters in a story to the best brand of pickles.

    The Gardener is a story written in the form of letters from a girl to her family. Since there is no narrator, we have to draw a lot of our own conclusions about the characters and the plot. As you read *The Gardener*, make sure you practice comparing and contrasting the characters, the setting, and the different parts of the plot.

THE Gardener

Sarah Stewart
Illustrated by David Small

August 27, 1935
Dear Uncle Jim,

Grandma told us after supper that you want me to come to the city and live with you until things get better. Did she tell you that Papa has been out of work for a long time, and no one asks Mama to make dresses anymore? We all cried, even Papa. But then Mama made us laugh with her stories about your chasing her up trees when you were both little. Did you really do that?

I'm small, but strong, and I'll help you all I can. However, Grandma said to finish my schoolwork before doing anything else.

Your niece,

Lydia Grace Finch

September 3, 1935

Dear Uncle Jim,

    I'm mailing this from the train station.
I forgot to tell you in the last letter *three important things* that I'm too shy to say to your face:

1. I know a lot about gardening, but nothing about baking.
2. I'm anxious to learn to bake, but is there any place to plant seeds?
3. I like to be called "Lydia Grace"—just like Grandma.

        Your niece,
        Lydia Grace Finch

On the train

September 4, 1935

Dear Mama,

I feel so pretty in your dress that you made over for me. I hope you don't miss it too much.

Dear Papa,

I haven't forgotten what you said about recognizing Uncle Jim: "Just look for Mama's face with a big nose and a mustache!" I promise not to tell him. (Does he have a sense of humor?)

And, dearest Grandma,

Thank you for the seeds. The train is rocking me to sleep, and every time I doze off, I dream of gardens.

Love to all,

Lydia Grace

September 5, 1935

Dear Mama, Papa, and Grandma,

I'm so excited!!!

There are window boxes here! They look as if they've been waiting for me, so now we'll both wait for spring.

And, Grandma, the sun shines down on the corner where I'll live and work.

Love to all,

Lydia Grace

P.S. Uncle Jim doesn't smile.

December 25, 1935

Dear Mama, Papa, and Grandma,

I adore the seed catalogues[1] you sent. And, Grandma, thank you for all the bulbs.[2] I hope you received my drawings.

I wrote a long poem for Uncle Jim. He didn't smile, but I think he liked it. He read it aloud, then put it in his shirt pocket and patted it.

Love to all,
Lydia Grace

---

1. *Seed catalogues* are pamphlets sent out by seed companies. They usually have the names of a variety of seeds; pictures of the grown tree, flower, fruit, or vegetable that will grow from each seed; the price of the seed; and the instructions for ordering seeds.
2. Not everything grows from seeds. Some plants, like tulips or onions, grow from small round *bulbs* that contain the food for the plant's growth.

February 12, 1936

Dearest Grandma,

Thank you again for those bulbs you sent. You should see them now!

I really like Ed and Emma Beech, Uncle Jim's friends who work here. When I first arrived, Emma told me she'd show me how to knead bread if I would teach her the Latin names of all the flowers I know. Now, just half a year later, I'm kneading bread and she's speaking Latin!

More good news: We have a store cat named Otis who at this very moment is sleeping at the foot of *my* bed.

Love to all,

Lydia Grace

P.S. Uncle Jim isn't smiling yet, but I'm hoping for a smile soon.

March 5, 1936

Dear Mama, Papa, and Grandma,

    I've discovered a secret place. You can't imagine how wonderful it is. No one else knows about it but Otis.

    I have great plans.

    Thank you for all the letters. I'll try to write more, but I'm really busy planting all your seeds in cracked teacups and bent cake pans! And, Grandma, you should smell the good dirt I'm bringing home from the vacant lot down the street.

            Love to all,
            Lydia Grace

April 27, 1936
Dearest Grandma,

All the seeds and roots are sprouting. I can hear you saying, "April showers bring May flowers."

Emma and I are sprucing up the bakery and I'm playing a great trick on Uncle Jim. He sees me reading my mail, planting seeds in the window boxes, going to school, doing my homework, sweeping the floor. But he never sees me working in my secret place.

Love to all,
Lydia Grace

P.S. I'm planning on a big smile from Uncle Jim in the near future.

May 27, 1936

Dear Mama, Papa, and Grandma,

You should have heard Emma laugh today when I opened your letter and dirt fell out onto the sidewalk! Thank you for all the baby plants. They survived the trip in the big envelope.

More about Emma: She's helping me with the secret place. Hurrah!

Love to all,

Lydia Grace

P.S. I saw Uncle Jim almost smile today. The store was full (well, *almost* full) of customers.

June 27, 1936

Dear Grandma,

    Flowers are blooming all over the place. I'm also growing radishes, onions, and three kinds of lettuce in the window boxes.

    Some neighbors have brought containers for me to fill with flowers, and a few customers even gave me plants from their gardens this spring! They don't call me "Lydia Grace" anymore. They call me "the gardener."

                Love to all,

                Lydia Grace

P.S. I'm sure Uncle Jim will smile soon. I'm almost ready to show him the secret place.

July 4, 1936

Dearest Mama, Papa, and Grandma,

I am bursting with happiness! The entire city seems so beautiful, especially this morning.

The secret place is ready for Uncle Jim. At noon, the store will close for the holiday, and then we'll bring him up to the roof.

I've tried to remember everything you ever taught me about beauty.

Love to all,
Lydia Grace

P.S. I can already imagine Uncle Jim's smile.

July 11, 1936

Dear Mama, Papa, and Grandma,

My heart is pounding so hard I'm sure the customers can hear it downstairs!

At lunch today, Uncle Jim put the "Closed" sign on the door and told Ed and Emma and me to go upstairs and wait. He appeared with the most amazing cake I've ever seen—covered in flowers!

I truly believe that cake equals one thousand smiles.

And then he took your letter out of his pocket with the news of Papa's job!

I'M COMING HOME!

Love to all, and see you soon,
Lydia Grace

P.S. Grandma, I've given all of my plants to Emma. I can't wait to help you in your garden again. We gardeners never retire.

ABOUT THE AUTHOR

Sarah Stewart grew up as a shy, quiet child in Texas. She loved gardening in her grandmother's garden and writing poetry or reading in a big closet at home. As an adult, she has five gardens that she tends all summer, and she spends the winter reading and writing in her library. Her husband, David Small, illustrates the books that she writes. Ms. Stewart and her husband live in Michigan with a cat named Mabel, who they say is in charge.

ABOUT THE ILLUSTRATOR

Though **David Small** has been drawing pictures from the age of two, he did not always know that he would become an artist. He hated the art lessons that he took as a child, though he enjoyed drawing cartoons. When he grew up, Mr. Small wanted to write plays, but in the middle of college, he switched to art, and there, he says, he "found a real home." Today, Mr. Small has won many awards for his work, and he says that illustrating children's picture books is the art he most enjoys. When he is not illustrating books, Mr. Small likes to swim, travel, and ride his bike.

Springtime

Nikki
Giovanni

in springtime the violets
grow in the sidewalk cracks
and the ants play furiously
at my gym-shoed toes
carrying off a half-eaten peanut
butter sandwich i had at lunch
and sometimes i crumble
my extra graham crackers
and on the rainy days i take off
my yellow space hat and splash
all the puddles on Pendry Street
and not one
cold can catch me

Studying the Selection

FIRST IMPRESSIONS

How would a young girl react to the news that she was being sent to live with an uncle she didn't know until the situation at home got better?

QUICK REVIEW

1. Why is Lydia Grace being sent to the city?

2. About what does Lydia Grace know a lot and about what does she know nothing?

3. What was the secret place that Lydia Grace wrote about in her letters?

4. How did Uncle Jim show how much he appreciated Lydia Grace?

FOCUS

5. Lydia Grace writes that her grandmother always says, "April showers bring May flowers." What is the lesson taught by that expression?

6. Compare Lydia Grace's grandmother with Lydia Grace. How are they alike? Contrast Lydia Grace with Uncle Jim. How are they different?

CREATING AND WRITING

7. All of the letters in *The Gardener* are written by Lydia Grace. We never see any of the letters written to Lydia Grace by her mother, father, or grandmother. Choose one of the letters in the story and write a response to it from the person to whom it was addressed.

8. Your teacher will ask each of you to bring something from home in which you can plant some seeds. As you know from reading the story, you can use almost anything as a flowerpot. Be creative in your choice. Your teacher will provide you with potting soil and seeds. In a short time, your classroom may look like Lydia Grace's secret place!

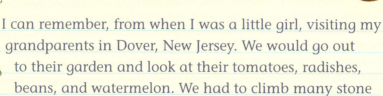

Jill's Journal:
On Assignment in Iowa

I can remember, from when I was a little girl, visiting my grandparents in Dover, New Jersey. We would go out to their garden and look at their tomatoes, radishes, beans, and watermelon. We had to climb many stone steps to see the grape arbor and a cherry tree. Both the tree and the grapes had been planted by my grandfather many years earlier.

I have been hearing interesting stories about the gardens families had during the Great Depression. The Great Depression occurred from about 1929 to 1939. It was a time when many thousands of Americans lost their jobs and had very little to eat.

I have read about a family in Iowa, the Beuschers, who before the Depression were doing very well, even with their eight children. Then Mr. Beuscher lost his job and hard times began. I have decided to go back to 1933 and see if I can visit them.

I had no way to let them know ahead of time that I was coming. I am standing now on their front porch, knocking on the door. Of course, I have dressed in the clothing people wore in the 1930s. Mrs. Beuscher, who is 54, answers my knock and smiles at me.

"Hello, Mrs. Beuscher. I know you don't know me, but my name is Jill and I am an investigative reporter. I would very much like to talk with you and your husband about how you are faring since your husband lost his job. I am interested in writing about the ways that people are managing. If you could just talk with me for a short time, I would be very grateful."

She welcomes me into the living room, where the sewing machine is open. There are several different kinds of fabric and a sewing pattern is pinned to some heavy cloth. "As you can see," she said, "this is one of the ways we manage. I make all of our clothes and also sell some of what I sew to neighbors and friends. I don't get much—because they haven't got money, either, but it's better than nothing."

Mr. Beuscher is sitting at the kitchen table, fixing one of the garden tools. "Come on in. You said your name is Jill? Well, come on in, Jill. I'm not sure how we are making it. I worked for 29 years at the railroad shops. When they closed, that was real hard for me. But the Mrs. sews best she can, and we got serious about having a vegetable garden. Also we got us some laying hens for the eggs, and we sell some of those."

Mrs. Beuscher adds, "We are fortunate that we have the apple trees out back. I can put up lots of applesauce, and we even sell some apples in the autumn."

"Where are all of those children of yours?" I ask.

"Oh," says Mrs. Beuscher, "Charles, Celia, Butch, Eileen—"

"Don't forget Caroline," interrupts Mr. Beuscher.

"How could I forget Caroline?" she laughs. "Well, those five children are already married and having their own hard time now. We tell them that if they need it, if they can't pay their rent, then they can come back home

with their families and somehow we'll make do. Only Paul, Katherine, and Jeannette are still at home. They're in school right now. They are very good kids and each of them has some sort of paying job. Even if they only make 15 cents a week, like our Paulie, they chip in. And every one of them helps with chores. We all work in the garden. Of course Pa does the most."

"Well, Mr. Beuscher, what do you grow?" I ask, curious.

"We've got tomatoes, carrots, onions, potatoes, cabbage, zucchini, and peppers. That's what does the best here. I have to be real careful about bugs and I can't miss a day of weeding. Got to admit it's hard on my back."

Mrs. Beuscher says, "I do a lot of canning. In fact, I can a little almost every day in the summer, just as the vegetables are ready for use. Last summer I put up 500 quarts of vegetables. That's what got us through the winter. What's extra, Katherine and Jeannette take door to door to sell in the summer and fall."

"Oh, and I just got us some beehives," Mr. Beuscher says enthusiastically. "That way we don't need the money to buy sugar if we have honey."

"What would you tell someone if you wanted to encourage them in a situation like this?" I ask.

Mr. Beuscher says that his wife always tells him to "stay hopeful, ask for guidance, and not to lose the joy of life." The Beuschers look at each other and smile.

POWER SKILL:
Conducting an Interview

As you can see from reading Jill's Journals, one of the ways we can learn about the past is to interview a person who lived at that time. (Another way is to read books about the past or to look at old newspapers.) Of course, you cannot travel back in time as Jill does, so if you are going to interview someone, he or she has to be someone who lives in the present time.

Developing interview skills can be really helpful. For this assignment, you will pick someone you know who is older and who has the time and interest to be asked about his or her earlier life.

An interview can be about nearly anything, as long as your questions are good and the person you interview is able to give detailed answers. You want to end up with more information than which you started.

Remember: Write down your questions before you begin. Don't forget to tell what your relationship is with the person you are interviewing. Tell that person how important it is to receive detailed answers.

Here are some ideas:

- What is your name?
- Who were the members of your family when you were a child?
- Describe an experience you had with your family as a child.
- What is your strongest memory from childhood?

5

wrap-up

all about theme!

unit

ACTIVITY ONE

People have some very strange pets! We can sometimes tell something about people by the pets they choose. For example, a lady with a beautiful French poodle probably likes pretty, dainty things. Someone who owns a pet alligator likes to live dangerously! Think about the main characters of each selection in this unit. Choose one of them and think of a pet for that person. On a sheet of paper, write the name of the character and selection you have chosen, and draw a picture of the pet you have imagined for this character. At the bottom of the page, write two sentences explaining why your chosen character would have this pet.

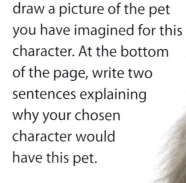

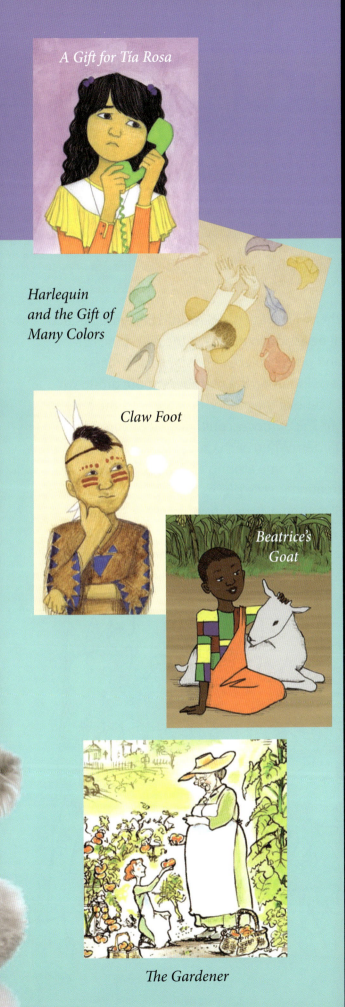

A Gift for Tía Rosa

Harlequin and the Gift of Many Colors

Claw Foot

Beatrice's Goat

The Gardener

ACTIVITY TWO

It is impossible for an author to write everything that a character in a story might feel. You, the reader, have to use your own imagination.

Here is a list of some situations in the Unit Five stories where the author leaves it to us to imagine how the character would feel. Write an answer to *one* of the questions that follow. Your teacher will call on you to read what you have written. Your answer should be two to four sentences long.

1. How did Carmela feel when she finished knitting the baby blanket for the new baby?
2. How did Harlequin feel about his costume, his friends, and the fun he had?
3. How did Broken Wing feel when he saw Claw Foot?
4. How did Beatrice feel as she sat in her new classroom?
5. How did Lydia Grace feel when she first arrived in the city and met her unsmiling uncle?

5 | wrap-up
continued

ACTIVITY THREE

Your teacher will divide the class into five groups. Each group will be assigned to one of the five stories in the unit and given a piece of poster board, markers, and scissors. Together, the members of the group will draw one scene of their story. For example, the group assigned to *The Gardener* could draw a picture of a rooftop garden. When each group's picture is done, the teacher will come around and draw lines over the picture, creating puzzle pieces. One member of the group will cut the picture into puzzle pieces, place the pieces in a box, and hand the box to a different group. When the teacher says "Go!" each group will race to put the puzzle together. The group that finishes first is the winner!

ACTIVITY FOUR

Each of the stories in this unit is about a young boy or girl. Each of these young people had a skill. Carmela could knit; Harlequin could dance; Claw Foot could ride a horse and hunt; Beatrice could farm, milk a goat, and run a small business; Lydia Grace could garden. Imagine that when these characters grew up, each was looking for a job using the skill we have mentioned. Pretend you are one of the characters. Write three short paragraphs and explain why you would be good for the job being offered. In the first paragraph, write what you think the job requires. In the second paragraph, write about your experience and skill in that area. For example, if you chose to be Lydia Grace looking for a job in a flower shop, you could start your first paragraph by saying a flower shop needs someone who understands how to grow plants. You would add one or two more requirements. In your next paragraph you would write where you, Lydia Grace, learned the skills you've mentioned.

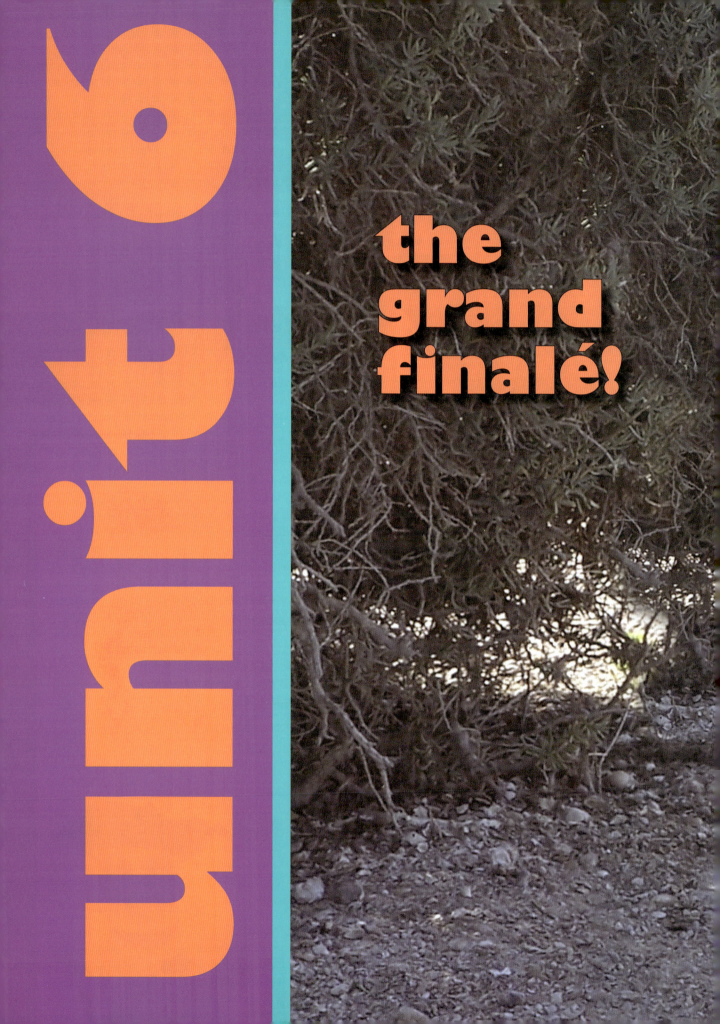

unit 6

the grand finalé!

Lesson in Literature...

THE RIGHT TO BE TREATED WELL

Every person wants to be treated well. In our neighborhoods, at school, in the factories, farms, schools, or offices where we work, every man, woman, and child looks for fairness and the chance for opportunity.

THE PURPOSE OF BIOGRAPHY

- A **biography** is the true story of a person's life.
- A biography tells us not only about the person, but also about the times in which the person lived.
- An author may write a biography to inform the reader about the life and times of a certain person.
- Another reason an author may write a biography is to inspire the reader by showing how much one individual can accomplish.

THINK ABOUT IT!

1. Why was Eleanor Roosevelt happier at the boarding school than she had been at her own home or at her grandmother's house?
2. What did Eleanor do when she completed school?
3. What important work did Eleanor do after her husband died?

Words very much like these were once written by a woman named Eleanor Roosevelt. She was the niece of President Theodore Roosevelt, and the wife and First Lady of President Franklin Roosevelt.

Eleanor Roosevelt grew up among very rich people. Her family had lived in New York from the 1600s and was very well-known. But as a child, Eleanor suffered many hurts.

Eleanor was shy and serious. Her mother called her 'Granny,' because she felt that Eleanor acted like an old lady and was very serious. This made Eleanor feel very bad. In fact, Eleanor felt ashamed that she was not more like her mother.

When Eleanor was eight, her mother died from a sickness called diphtheria. (Today, babies are inoculated against this illness.) The same winter, the older of her two younger brothers died of scarlet fever and diphtheria. Two years later, her father died. Eleanor was just ten years old. She was moved to her grandmother's house, a busy place where no one had time for her. Eleanor led a lonely life there.

People came and went at Grandmother's and she had little privacy. So when she was 15, her aunt enrolled her in a boarding school near London. Eleanor loved this school. There, people thought that what was important about a young woman was how she used her mind. Her boarding school was a place where the things that she thought were important—like helping people who needed help—also mattered to her friends and teachers.

Eleanor Roosevelt would spend most of her life trying to make other people's lives better.

When she returned to the U.S., still a teenager, she began working in the slums at a settlement house. This was very unusual for a rich, young woman. A settlement house was a neighborhood center that provided medical care and food for the poor, and helped immigrants with classes for grownups and children and with training for jobs.

The young Eleanor said, "There is joy in accomplishing good."

Eleanor Roosevelt married Franklin Roosevelt and they had six children in eleven years. Her husband was first elected governor of New York and then, in 1932, became the president of the United States. As First Lady, she worked for equal rights for all Americans. Each year, Mrs. Roosevelt was called upon to make more than seventy speeches. She wrote 2,500 newspaper columns and published six books.

In 1939, a well-known organization wouldn't let Marian Anderson perform in Constitution Hall because she was black. Mrs. Roosevelt arranged for Mrs. Anderson to appear at the Lincoln Memorial. This took great courage in those days. Seventy-five thousand people attended.

When her husband, the president, became ill with polio and was paralyzed, Eleanor was there to take care of him— just as she was there during World War II, visiting the troops and the wounded in hospitals.

In April 1945, President Roosevelt died. After the loss of her husband, Eleanor continued to work tirelessly for others. She helped to create a document called the Universal Declaration of Human Rights. Because she spoke up for the rights of people around the globe, she became known as "The First Lady of the World." From her shy and humble beginnings, Eleanor Roosevelt became one of the most admired women in American history. She was a woman of grace and wisdom.

Blueprint for Reading

INTO . . . *Rocks in His Head*

The world is full of so many things—and somebody, somewhere, is fascinated by each one of them! What may be of no interest to you is thrilling to somebody else, and what draws you like a magnet may put your friend to sleep. The father in this story loves rocks. From the time he was a boy, he studied, collected, traded, and displayed unusual rocks. As an adult, he had different jobs, but his true interest was always rocks. People teased him and said he had "rocks in his head," but he just smiled good-naturedly and showed them his latest find. As you read *Rocks in His Head*, you may be surprised to find that you, too, have begun to be curious about rocks. That's because excitement about anything—even rocks—is contagious!

EYES ON *The Purpose of Biography*

The reason the author wrote the story is called the **author's purpose**. When the story is a *biography*, the author clearly feels it is important that you learn about a certain person. What does the author want you to learn? That all depends on the person being written about. The story may make you laugh, or cry, or think about something new. It may amaze you or upset you. Most often, someone writes a biography to inspire you. As you read *Rocks in His Head*, ask yourself, which of these was the author's purpose?

Rocks in His Head

Carol Otis Hurst

Some people collect stamps. Some people collect coins or dolls or bottle caps. When he was a boy, my father collected rocks. When he wasn't doing chores at home or learning at school, he'd walk along stone walls and around old quarries, looking for rocks. People said he had rocks in his pockets and rocks in his head.[1] He didn't mind. It was usually true.

When people asked what he wanted to be when he grew up, he'd say, "Something to do with rocks, I think."

1. The expression *rocks in his head* means "a little crazy."

"There's no money in rocks," someone said.

"Probably not," said my father.

When he grew up, my father decided to open a gas station. (People called them filling stations then.) My grandfather helped him build one on Armory Street in Springfield, Massachusetts.

They called the station the Antler Filling Station. My father carefully painted the name right over the doorway.

Inside the filling station was a desk with a cash drawer (which my father usually forgot to lock) and a table for his chess set.

My father built narrow wooden shelves on the back wall and painted them white. People said, "What are those shelves for?"

He said, "I've got rocks in my head, I guess."

Then, one by one, he placed his rocks and minerals on those shelves. He carefully labeled each rock to show what kind it was and where it had come from.

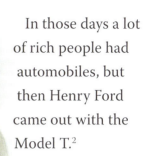

In those days a lot of rich people had automobiles, but then Henry Ford came out with the Model T.[2]

That was a car many people could afford. My father had taken one apart and put it back together again and again until he knew every inch of the Model T. He thought that anyone who had spare parts for the Model T and could repair it so that it drove like new would do a good business. He bought some parts from dealers and found some parts in junkyards.

The pile of Model T parts sat just to the left of the lift. Soon, that pile of parts was bigger than the filling station.

People said, "If you think people are going to buy that junk, you've got rocks in your head."

"Maybe I have," he said. "Maybe I have."

---

2. The *Model T* was the first car produced that the average person could afford.

> ## WORD BANK
>
> **lift** *n.*: a device found in mechanics' garages that can lift cars several feet off the ground

But people did come and buy that junk. They came to buy gas, and they came to play chess, and they came to look at the rocks.

For a while my father was too busy for the chess games. He was pumping gas, changing tires, and fixing Model Ts.

"Where did you get this one?" a customer would say, holding up a rock.

"Found it in a slag pile[3] in New Hampshire," he'd say. Or, "Traded for it with a fella from Nevada. Gave him some garnets from Connecticut."

"People in Nevada and Connecticut collect rocks like you do?" people would ask.

"Lots of folks have rocks in their heads," said my father. He'd dig into his pocket and take out a rock. "Take a look at this one."

Then the stock market fell. At first, people didn't think it would matter much to my father. After all, he had no money in the stock market.

"I may have rocks in my head," he said, "but I think bad times are coming."

And bad times did come. People couldn't afford to buy new cars or fix their old ones.

---

3. Some metals are found in a rocklike substance called ore. When the metal is separated from the ore, the leftover material is called *slag*. A *slag pile* is a pile of useless, rocky material.

WORD BANK

garnets (GAR nets) *n.*: a semiprecious stone that is a deep red color

When business was slow, my father would play chess with some of his customers. When business was very slow, my grandfather would mind the filling station, and we'd pile as many of us kids as would fit into our Model T, and we'd hunt for more rocks with my father. He had to build more shelves for the rocks, up the west wall of the station.

Then people stopped coming for gas. They stopped coming to play chess, and they even stopped coming to look at the rocks and minerals. They were all too busy looking for work.

One day my father picked up the chess set and carefully packed it in a big box. He took down each mineral, wrapped it in newspaper, and carefully placed it in a wooden box.

When his friends came with a truck to help us move, they said, "Watch out for those wooden boxes. He's got rocks in his boxes, now."

"Yessir," said my father. "That's just what I got in there. Take a look at this one."

The house we moved to was old and falling apart. My father said he'd have it fixed up in no time.

But before he started in on the repairs, we had to take those rocks up to the attic, where he'd already built tiny little wooden shelves.

My father did fix up the old house, and after he finished each repair, he went up to the attic with his rocks. He spent a lot of time reading about rocks, too.

"If you think those rocks are ever going to do you any good," said my mother, "you've got rocks in your head."

"Maybe I have," said my father. "Maybe I have." He reached into his pocket. "Take a look at this one."

My father spent a lot of time looking for any job he could find. Most jobs lasted only a day or two.

On rainy days when my father could find no other work, he'd take the bus to the science museum. They had a whole room full of glass cases containing many rocks. Sometimes he'd spend the whole day in that room.

One afternoon he looked up to see a lady standing beside him. "I've seen you here before," she said.

"I come here a lot," he said. "I guess I've got rocks in my head."

"Tell me what you're looking for," she said.

"I'm looking for rocks that are better than mine," he said.

"How many did you find?" she asked.

"Ten," he said.

The lady looked around at the hundreds of rocks, in all those glass cases. "Only ten?"

"Maybe eleven," he said.

He smiled. She did, too.

"You *have* got rocks in your head," she said. "I'm Grace Johnson, the director of this museum. These rocks have come from all over the world."

"So have mine," said my father. He reached into his pocket. "Take a look at this one," he said.

"Did you study rocks at college?" she asked.

"Couldn't afford to go to college," he said.

"Let me see the rest of your rocks," she said.

Mrs. Johnson got out her big Packard touring car, and my father got in. They drove to our house.

"Where are the rocks?" she asked.

"Up here," said my father, leading the way to the attic. "Watch your step."

Two hours later Mrs. Johnson said, "I can't hire you as a mineralogist. The board won't allow it. But I need a night janitor at the museum. Will you take the job?"

"Will I be cleaning rocks?" he asked.

"Sometimes," she said.

So my father took the job as night janitor at the museum. Before he went home, he'd open some of the mineral cases and scrub some of the rocks with a toothbrush until they sparkled like diamonds.

Mrs. Johnson came in early for work one morning and saw him carefully writing a new label for one of the rocks.

"What are you doing?" she asked.

"One rock was labeled wrong," he said. "I fixed it."

Mrs. Johnson smiled. "I've been talking to the board of directors. They know that I need a person here who knows as much about rocks as you do."

"What about the college education?" he asked.

She said, "I told them I need somebody with rocks in his head and rocks in his pockets. Are you it?"

"Maybe I am," said my father. "Maybe I am."

CURATOR[4] OF MINERALOGY

He reached into his pocket and took out a rock.

"Take a look at this one," he said.

---

4. A *curator* is the person in charge of one of the museum's collections. The *Curator of Mineralogy* is the person in charge of the museum's collection of minerals.

ABOUT THE AUTHOR

Carol Otis Hurst said that her father was an "amazing man." She told his story to her children because "they never knew my father but they tripped over rocks in boxes all over the place." She began telling it at workshops, and eventually wrote it down for her grandchildren. Mrs. Hurst worked as a teacher, school librarian, storyteller, educational consultant, and workshop director before she started writing children's books. When Mrs. Hurst was in her sixties, *Rocks in His Head* finally became a book.

Studying the Selection

QUICK REVIEW

1. What was the father's first job?

2. What happened to the father's business and the family's house when the "bad times" came?

3. What did the father build in the new house? Why?

4. What did the father do in his spare time when he could not find work?

FOCUS

5. Why was the father willing to take a job as janitor at the museum?

6. The author clearly loved her father. Write about two of her father's personality traits that you think she especially admired.

CREATING AND WRITING

7. Imagine that you are Mrs. Johnson, trying to persuade the board of directors to appoint the father, who does not have a college education, to be curator of mineralogy at the museum. Write a letter that starts with the heading, "Dear Members of the Board of Directors," and write two paragraphs that explain why the father would make a good curator of mineralogy. Sign the letter, "Sincerely, Mrs. Johnson."

8. Now is your chance to share your hobby or collection with your classmates. Bring your stamps or rocks or miniature china dolls or whatever collection you have to school on the appointed day. If you have a hobby that cannot be displayed, write a paragraph about what you do in your spare time and read it to the class when your teacher calls on you. If your hobby is reading, for example, you may want to tell the class about the latest book you have read.

Lesson in Literature ...
PICO GOES HOME

REALITY AND FANTASY

- A **realistic story** is a story that did not happen but that could have happened.
- A story that is **fantasy** tells about events that could not happen in the real world.
- Some stories are a mix of reality and fantasy.
- At times, an author will make it difficult to tell whether or not something in the story really happened or was only a fantasy.

THINK ABOUT IT!

1. What were some of the mean things Pico's owners did to him?
2. Where did Pico finally find some food?
3. Some parts of this story are real and some are fantasy. What happens in the story that is fantasy?

Pico stood outdoors in the light of the streetlamp. He was shivering in the cold. It was January, and there was a sheet of ice on the ground. It felt as though his paws were starting to freeze. He was a little dog, and his ribs stuck out.

The people who had bought him at the awful pet store had done a lot of yelling. They were very impatient when they walked him. He loved to sniff the bushes and grass on his walks. The smells made pictures in his head of the animals who had been there before him: a cat, another dog, a raccoon, an opossum. For him, sniffing was like reading a book.

His owners had not allowed much sniffing and had spent most of the walk dragging him away from every good smell. They did not pet him. He was never allowed to lie next to them on the couch or sleep under the soft blankets. They had a little boy who did mean things to him.

Then, one night, they had pushed him out the door and wouldn't let him back in. He had sat near the door for a very long time. But the door had never opened to his cries. He had gotten so cold. The next morning he left.

He had walked and walked. He didn't know where he was going. He didn't know where to go. He had seen some families and run towards them. The children had called out to him. But their parents said, "Stay away from that filthy dog! He might have rabies!" Pico was shocked by these words. He had always been such a clean dog and so well-behaved.

Pico felt like giving up. A river ran through the middle of the city and he walked down a path to the river's edge. No one seemed to remember that a dog was man's best friend. He tried to step into the water, but it was frozen and he just slid on the ice. He walked back up the path, away from the river.

He found himself in a different neighborhood. He noticed that plastic bags of trash were out in front of each of the houses on this street. He started to sniff each bag and search frantically for something to eat. He knew it was bad manners, but he tore open a bag that smelled promising. It was an old, frozen bone, but it had a little meat on it. He dragged it under a nearby porch and gnawed on it.

He had fallen asleep after chewing on the bone. Sleep was a blessing because when he was asleep, he didn't remember. When he awoke, it had begun to snow. Pico noticed that the houses here were very big. Maybe one of the big houses would have room for a little dog.

He didn't know where to wait or how to make himself cleaner. He rolled in the snow. Maybe that would work. But this made him colder, because the snow melted and got his fur wet. Then he saw someone tall walking down the street in the dark night. Quickly, he wrote with the point of his nose in the snow, "Please take me home with you." The man approached, bent down, and petted him. The man almost thought he saw letters in the snow. "Oh, you poor little dog," he said. "Where is your collar?"

He picked Pico up and walked over to the light of the streetlamp. He could see how starved Pico was. "Oh my, you do need food! Well, I don't know what people will say at home, but I can't leave you." He wrapped his scarf around Pico. Then the man unzipped his jacket a bit and tucked the little dog down into the opening. Pico's head stuck up from the jacket. He sniffed the cold air with his pointy nose. *I'm going home*, he thought. *I can't believe it, but I'm going home.*

Blueprint for Reading

INTO . . . *The Naming of Olga da Polga*

How important is your name? Is it just a label and you are you, no matter what people call you? Or is it part of who you are, and you would not be the same person if you had another name? People have different answers to this question. Some people even change their names because they don't like their given names. Others are offended if people use a nickname for them or mispronounce their name. In short, people's feelings about their names are very individual. As you read *The Naming of Olga da Polga*, you will see how one very human guinea pig feels about having her name changed. Would you feel as strongly?

EYES   ON   *Fantasy*

A **fantasy** is something you can imagine but could not happen in the real world. Volcanoes that gush chocolate milk or flowers that talk are fantasies. Some stories are full of fantasy. Other stories are completely realistic. But there are some stories that mix fantasy and reality. As you read, you, the reader, have to jump between the two. And you do! Something in your mind tells you, "this is real," and "this is not." But—authors can be tricky! Sometimes they write one part of the story that leaves you wondering: Did this happen or was it just the character's imagination? As you read *The Naming of Olga da Polga*, try to find the place in the story where the author plays that trick!

THE NAMING OF
Olga da Polga

A story from *The Tales of Olga da Polga* by Michael Bond

Olga da Polga was not just an ordinary guinea pig. She was a smart, daring guinea pig who just knew that one day soon she would leave the crowded pet shop and see the world. One day, a man and a small girl came to the shop to buy a pet. As soon as the girl saw Olga, she pointed at her and said, "That's the one!"

Before she knew it, Olga was put into a cardboard box and was on her way to the girl's house. On the way there, she heard the man tell the girl that he had built a marvelous cage with a wood roof, a glass window, and a wire net door. "It sounds like a palace," thought Olga da Polga.

If Olga da Polga's new home wasn't exactly a palace it certainly seemed like it, and it was definitely the nearest she was ever likely to get to one.

After the cramped and crowded conditions in the pet shop it was like entering a different world.

The hutch was large and airy and it was divided into two halves. Both floors were neatly covered with sawdust and the rooms were separated by a wall which had a hole cut in the middle so that she could easily pass between the two.

The first half was a kind of all-purpose room, part dining room, part playroom. The room had a wire mesh door, a small ash branch in one corner so that Olga could keep her teeth nice and sharp, and two heavy bowls—one marked OATS and the other marked WATER.

Olga tried out both before turning her attention to the second room. This turned out to be even more exciting than the first, for it not only had a *glass window* to keep out the weather, but there was a large, inviting mound of fresh-smelling hay as well.

Olga spent some time pressing the hay flat so that she would have somewhere comfortable to sleep without being too hot, and then she settled down to think things over.

Really, all things considered, life had taken a very pleasant turn.

The sun was shining. The birds were chirping. Even the noises seemed friendly. Olga enjoyed the clinkings, singing, and occasional humming sounds from somewhere inside the big house as Mr. and Mrs. Sawdust—which was what Olga had decided to call them—went about their work.

Every so often there was a reassuring murmur of voices outside as one or other of the family peered through the glass to make certain she was all right.

WORD BANK

considered (kun SID erd) *adj.*: thought about

reassuring (REE uh SHUR ing) *adj.*: giving one confidence

First came Mr. Sawdust, then Mrs. Sawdust, then some other people called "neighbors" and they all had a friendly word or two to say to her.

Finally Karen Sawdust herself arrived with an enormous pile of grass, a bunch of dandelions, and a large juicy carrot neatly sliced down the center, which she placed temptingly alongside the feeding bowl.

"We're going to choose a name for you now," Karen announced, as Olga stirred herself and came out of the bedroom to sample these new delicacies. "And we have to make sure it's right because tomorrow Daddy's going to paint it over your front door. There'll be no changing it once that's done."

Olga nibbled away, half listening, half in a world of her own.

"Daddy fancies Greta and Mummy's rather keen on Gerda, but I'm not sure. They don't sound *special* enough to me." Karen Sawdust put her face against the door as she turned to go. "I do wish you could tell us what *you* would like for a name."

"Greta? … Gerda? … *Painted on my front door*?" Olga's world suddenly turned upside down.

She paused, a carefully folded piece of grass half in, half out of her mouth, hardly able to believe her ears.

"But I'm Olga da Polga," she wailed, addressing the empty air. "I've always been Olga da Polga. I can't change now—I really can't." That night, long after darkness fell and everyone else had gone to bed, Olga was still wide awake and deep in thought.

"I suppose," she said to herself, for what seemed like the hundredth time, "I suppose I ought to be counting my blessings instead of grumbling. I mean, I have a nice new home … food … I'm among friends … but I *would* like to keep my own name, especially as I'm having it painted on."

The more Olga thought about it the sadder she became, for she couldn't help remembering a remark one of the older inhabitants of the pet shop had once made. "Always hang on to your name," he had said. "It may not be much, but when you're a guinea pig it's sometimes all you have in the world."

Olga's own name was firmly imprinted on her mind. OLGA DA POLGA.

It had taken her fancy straight away and now she had become so used to it she couldn't begin to picture having anything else. When she closed her eyes she could still see it written in large black letters on the side of an old cardboard box.

WORD BANK

inhabitants (in HAB ih tunts) *n.*: the people or animals who live in a place

Suddenly she jumped up in excitement, her mind in a whirl. Could she? Was it possible?

It would mean a lot of hard work. A lot of difficult, almost impossible work. And yet …

Getting out of her warm bed, shivering partly with the chill of the night air and partly with she knew not what, Olga made her way through into the next room.

Clutching the ash branch firmly in her mouth she set to work. Scratching and scraping, starting and stopping, she worked and she worked and she worked. Sometimes pausing to smooth the sawdust over before beginning all over again, she tried not once, but time after time and still it wouldn't come right.

Dawn was breaking before she crawled back into her bedroom at long last and sank down in the hay. Her paws were aching, her fur was covered in sawdust, and her eyes were so tired she could hardly bear to keep them open.

"It looks plain enough to me," she thought, gazing back at the result of her night's work, "but then, I *know* what it's meant to be. I only hope the others understand as well."

Gradually, as she enjoyed her well-earned rest, the air began to fill with sounds of morning. They were strange, unaccustomed sounds. In place of the usual grunts and rustles of the pet shop there were dogs barking, clocks striking, the sound of bottles clinking, and somewhere in the distance the noise of a train rattling on its way. In fact, there were so many different noises Olga soon lost count of them.

And then, at long last, came the one she had been waiting for. There was a click, the clatter of a bolt being withdrawn, and a moment later a now familiar face appeared on the other side of the wire netting.

In the pause which followed, Olga could almost hear the beating of her own heart.

"Mummy! Mummy!" With a shriek of surprise the face vanished from view. "Come quickly! Come and see!"

WORD BANK
gradually (GRAD ju uh lee) *adv.*: slowly but surely
unaccustomed (UN uh KUST umd) *adj.*: unusual
withdrawn (with DRAWN) *v.*: pulled back
vanished (VAN ishd) *v.*: disappeared

Olga jumped to her feet. "Wheeee! It's worked! It's worked! Wheeeeeee!" Squeaking with joy and pleasure at her own cleverness she ran round and round her dining room, scattering sawdust and the result of her labors in one wild whirlwind of delight.

"Olga da Polga?" exclaimed the voice of Mrs. Sawdust. "Written on the floor? Don't be silly … how *could* it have been?"

A face appeared at Olga's door. "I can't see anything at all. You must have been dreaming. All the same"—there was a pause—"it *is* a rather nice name. If I were you I'd keep it."

When they were alone again, Olga looked out of her window at Karen Sawdust and Karen Sawdust looked back at her.

"Grownups!" said Karen with a sigh. "They *never* understand these things. Still, we know it happened, don't we?"

Olga da Polga lifted up her head proudly. "Wheeee!" she cried, in the loudest voice she could possibly manage. "Wheeee! Wheeee! Wheeeeeeeee!"

And really, there was nothing more to be said.

ABOUT THE AUTHOR

Michael Bond says that he "grew up in a home where books were almost part of the furniture" and he "was read to almost as soon as [he] could recognize sounds." As a child, he enjoyed playing with spinning tops, iron hoops, and roller blades. Today, the list of the books he wrote fills pages. Mr. Bond is most famous for creating Paddington the bear, but he says that in a way, Olga is more interesting than Paddington. Most of his material for books comes from his own life and observations, and Olga is actually based on Mr. Bond's daughter's guinea pig.

QUICK REVIEW

1. How did Olga's new home compare to her old one at the pet shop?

2. What had the owners placed in the first room of Olga's cage?

3. What did Karen tell Olga that upset Olga tremendously?

4. How did Olga "tell" Karen what her real name was?

FOCUS

5. Did Mummy believe that Olga had written her name on the floor? Why or why not?

6. This story is a mix of reality and fantasy. Write down two events or descriptions that could be true and two that could only happen in an imaginary world.

CREATING AND WRITING

7. Many names have meanings. They may be taken from English, like "Smith," or foreign languages, like "Schumacher," for shoemaker. Look at the name Olga da Polga. What does it mean? Use your imagination and sense of humor and, in two or three sentences, explain what the name means!

8. Your teacher will divide your class into groups and assign each group an unusual word or name. Each group will have to communicate this name to the rest of the class without saying the name directly or writing it out in the ordinary way. The groups will be given a few moments to brainstorm. They may choose to make up a pantomime, draw a set of pictures, or use other creative ways to help the class guess what name they were given.

Lesson in Literature . . .

HELPFUL LITTLE BEARS

USING DIALOGUE

- **Dialogue** is what the characters say in a story or play.
- The dialogue tells us what the characters are thinking.
- The dialogue tells us what is happening in the plot.
- The dialogue reveals the theme of the story.

THINK ABOUT IT!

1. Why are the bears preparing a special dinner?
2. Why does the dough rise so much?
3. What is one of Mama Bear's outstanding personality traits?

Inside the log cabin in the woods everyone was bustling. Papa Bear was coming home tonight. Mama Bear and the little bears, Jason, Melissa, and Benny, were helping Mama get ready for Papa's return.

"Now, we want this dinner to be really special," said Mama Bear.

"Yes," said Jason, the big brother in the house. "Papa's been gone for a whole week!"

"We'll help!" said his sister, Melissa, eagerly.

"Brrrr," said Benny. "It's cold in here."

"That's because there are so many cracks between the logs," said Jason. "The cold wind just comes right through the walls!"

"No complaining, kids," said Mama Bear. "Let's get going on this dinner!"

Mama went to the cupboard and took out flour, salt, oil, sugar, and yeast. The kids stood around her as she put ingredients for bread into her big baking bowl.

"Let's see," she said. "A cup of water, one teaspoon of salt, three teaspoons of sugar, and four cups of flour."

"I'll put in the yeast," said Melissa.

"Okay," said Mama Bear, turning to wash out the cups and spoons.

Melissa looked at the recipe. This is what she saw:

2 t. yeast

She measured out two tablespoons of yeast and put them in the bowl on top of the flour.

"I'll add some extra to make sure the bread is light and fluffy," she said to Jason.

"I'm done, Mama," she said.

"That was two teaspoons of yeast, right?" said Mama.

Melissa looked at Jason and Jason looked at Melissa. They both looked at the bowl. Neither said a word.

And now for the potatoes," said Mama. "Jason, cut up some potatoes and put them in the oven. Let's put the salmon into the pot and cook it."

"Bears love salmon," said Benny.

"They sure do!" said Jason, as he put a little salt on the salmon, then went to look at the dough. Benny grabbed the salt shaker and started pouring salt on the salmon. Mama turned around and saw him.

"Benny!" she said in alarm. "What are you doing?"

"Salting the salmon, Mama," said Benny smiling proudly. "See, I'm big enough to help with the cooking."

Mama did not want to hurt Benny's feelings, so she looked at the very, very salty salmon, smiled, and said, "Do you know what salty salmon is called? It's called lox. And your Papa just loves lox! Thank you, Benny!"

In the meantime, the dough was rising, and rising …

"What's burning?" asked Melissa.

"Oh, no!" cried Jason. "The potatoes burned!" He looked so sad that, had he not remembered he was eight years old, he would have cried.

Mama looked at his sad face. "Oh, honey," she said. "I'm so glad the potatoes are well-baked. Now we can add barbecue sauce and have barbequed potatoes, just like Papa loves."

Jason smiled and said, "I love them, too. That's why I wanted the potatoes to get that smoky taste."

Suddenly, everyone was quiet, even Benny. They were listening to a soft bubbly sound that filled the room. They looked at the mixing bowl in amazement as wet, sticky dough bubbled and oozed over the bowl, the counter, and onto the floor.

"What will we do with all that dough?" yelled the kids.

Mama thought for a minute. It would be some job pulling all that sticky dough off the countertop and floor. And then, she'd have to throw it out. What a waste! She shivered in the cold room.

"Children," she said. "I don't know why the dough rose like that, but this is going to be the best surprise of all. Now, each of you take some of the sticky dough and fill up every single crack in the wall with it."

When Papa came home, the table sparkled with its white tablecloth and shiny silverware.

"I'm home!" shouted Papa as the kids ran to the door. "Mmm, what smells so delicious? Are we having a barbeque? And, wait—it's really warm and cozy in here! Did you get a heater? Mama, how have these little bears been behaving while I was away? Did they help you?"

"Oh," said Mama Bear, "you would not believe how they helped!"

"Really?" said Papa. And he took all three bears in his arms and gave them a big bear hug.

Blueprint for Reading

INTO . . . *A Toad for Tuesday*

Did you ever have a countdown to something you dreaded? One week to complete a report you haven't started. Three days until your bossy cousin's visit. Ten minutes until your parents come home and see the broken window. What if you were a toad that was going to be eaten next Tuesday? What would you do? Is there anything you *could* do? A great man once said, "Never, never, never, never give up!" As you read *A Toad for Tuesday*, you will see what one small toad does to keep from being somebody's Tuesday night dinner.

EYES ON *Dialogue*

How do people get to know you? How do you share your thoughts? How do you make plans with other people? How do you get and give information? Mostly, by what you say and how you say it. In a story, what the characters say is called **dialogue**. The author uses dialogue to tell the reader about the characters, the plot, and the theme. As you read *A Toad for Tuesday*, notice the dialogue. It will tell you a lot about Morton, Warton, and the owl and how each of them thinks and feels.

A Toad
for
Tuesday

By RUSSELL E. ERICKSON

Illustrations by LAWRENCE DI FIORI

PART ONE

On a windy, wintry night, as countless stars were shining bright, deep in the ground, far under the snow, two little toads were having an argument. The two toads lived by themselves in their cozy home. Warton did the cleaning, and Morton did the cooking. Both did their jobs well, and it was, in fact, Morton's marvelous cooking that had started the argument.

After finishing a huge supper they settled back to enjoy dessert. As Morton poured a cup of clover-blossom tea Warton said, "This is the finest beetle brittle I have ever eaten."

"Thank you," Morton replied.

Then Warton said, "I'll bet dear old Aunt Toolia would surely love some."

"She certainly would," agreed Morton.

Warton said, "I'm going to put some in a box and take it to her this week."

> ## WORD BANK
>
> **countless** (KOWNT less)
> *adj.*: a large number of
> something; too many to count

At that, Morton spilled his hot tea all over himself and jumped so high he bounced off the ceiling. "Why, that's the most ridiculous idea I've ever heard!" he sputtered.

"Why?" said Warton.

"Because," said Morton, "it is winter up there." He pointed towards the crack in the ceiling he had just made, "And it is cold up there, and there is snow up there, but there is one thing you will not find up there—and that's another toad."

When he saw how long Warton's face had grown he was sorry he had spoken so harshly. "Warton," he said, "it's very kind of you to think of it, and it would be a fine idea except for two things. First, you would freeze and second, you would not be able to hop through all that deep snow."

Warton sighed, clasped his fingers and leaned far back. Morton could see that he was beginning to think. Whenever Warton thought about something he blinked his eyes—one at a time. They began to blink now, slowly at first, then faster, and then faster, and even faster, until suddenly

WORD BANK

sputtered (SPUH terd) *v.*: made explosive, popping sounds

a big grin appeared on his face. "I know how I shall do it," he cried.

"And how is that?" asked Morton.

"Well, so that I don't freeze, I'll wear four of my heaviest coats, three of my most tightly-knit sweaters, two pairs of my thickest mittens and my warm cap with the ear flaps. And to go through the snow … I'll make some skis."

"Skis? What are skis?" said Morton.

"Something a traveling rabbit told me about last summer, and I know just how to make them."

Morton's jaw dropped open, but he didn't say a word. He knew that once Warton's mind was made up there was no changing it.

For the next three days Warton worked very hard. He made his skis from strong oak tree roots. When he was done they were as handsome a pair of skis as anyone could want. They were sturdy and straight and polished to such a smoothness they felt like silk. He had also made ski poles to push with from porcupine quills and salamander leather.

On Wednesday morning he was ready to leave for Aunt Toolia's. It took quite a while to bundle up in all his warm clothes. The last thing he put on was a little pack Morton had made for him. In it were several lunches, for it would be at least three or four days' travel to Aunt Toolia's home. There were also a few other things which Warton thought he might need, such as an extra pair

WORD BANK

sturdy (STUR dee) *adj.*: strong and solid

of mittens and furry slippers. And on the bottom was the box of beetle brittle for Aunt Toolia.

He said goodbye to his brother who was already washing the breakfast dishes.

"Goodbye," said Morton, "and be very, very careful."

Warton started up through the long tunnel that led to the top of the old stump they lived under. When he stepped out he was dazzled. The brilliant snow glistened and glittered, and the deep blue sky was filled with puffy white clouds that drifted over the tall evergreens. Snowbirds twittered gaily as they hopped from branch to branch.

"This is positively beautiful," thought Warton. "But I must be going. It's a long way to Aunt Toolia's, and I'm curious to try my new skis."

He reached down and strapped them on and then gave a strong push. Immediately, the skis became tangled, sending him tumbling into a hill of snow. He hopped up quickly and tried again. This time he went much farther, until he ran

straight into a squirrel who was digging in the snow. Once again he hopped up, and after apologizing, off he went again.

Now he was going along quite well. The more he skied the more he enjoyed it. All bundled up in his four coats, three sweaters, two pairs of mittens, and his cap with the ear flaps, the little toad looked like a tiny ball skimming over the woodland snow.

After he had gone quite a way and when the sun was directly overhead he decided to have some lunch. He saw a perfect place to eat—a large, flat stump sticking out of the snow.

Stepping out of his skis and giving a big jump, he landed on top. He brought out one of his lunches and poured some hot acorn tea. He ate two sandwiches and was just about to bite into a slice of mosquito pie when he heard a strange sound.

It sounded very much like a far-off hiccup. Warton looked around, but he saw nothing. He started to take another bite and again he heard it. This time it seemed to come from below the stump. He hopped over to the edge and cautiously peeked down.

There, sticking out of the snow, were two furry brown legs with tiny white feet and little toes that wiggled and jiggled every time the hiccup was heard. Warton hopped down and began clearing away the snow as fast as he could. When he was

WORD BANK

cautiously (KAW shus lee) *adv.*: carefully and a bit anxiously

done he found that he had uncovered a brown and white furred deer-mouse. His big dark mouse eyes were filled with gratitude.

"Oh, thank you," the mouse said with relief. "That was … hic … most uncomfortable. It seems that whenever I become upside down I get the hiccups. I was afraid I would remain that way till the snow melts in the spring."

"How did you manage to get stuck upside down?" asked Warton with a blink.

"I was on top of the … hic … stump having a little snooze in the noon sun as I often do. But this time … hic … I had a dream that I was a merry-go-round, and before I could wake up I rolled right off the edge of the stump."

"I think I have just the thing for you," Warton said, "if you'll hop back up with me."

When they did, Warton gave the mouse some hot tea and right away the hiccups disappeared.

"Thank you again," said the mouse. "That's much better."

"You're very welcome," said Warton. "Do you live near here, by the way?"

> **WORD BANK**
>
> **gratitude** (GRAT ih tood) *n*.: appreciation; thankfulness
>
> **snooze** *n*.: a short nap

"As near as can be," said the mouse. "I live in this stump. And if I may ask, what is a toad like you doing out in the winter time?"

Warton told him about the beetle brittle for Aunt Toolia and how he was traveling on skis. The mouse thought it was a fine idea, but when Warton pointed in the direction in which he was going the mouse's eyes opened wide in dismay.

"Oh, you mustn't go through the wooded valley!" he cried.

"Why?" asked Warton with a blink.

The mouse leaned closer. "Because there is a certain owl who lives there," he said in a whisper. "Of all the owls in the world, I am sure that that one is the meanest and nastiest of them all. He is so sneaky that he hunts in the daytime when other owls sleep."

"But," said Warton, "I'll have to go through that valley, for if I go any other way I'll surely get lost. But don't worry," he said with a confident smile, "with my new skis I'll dash through that valley so fast the owl will never catch me."

"Then you wait here a moment," said the mouse, and he scampered down the side of the stump and disappeared into a hole. When he returned he had a round box with him. Out of it he took a small scarf. It was colored a most unusual and pretty red. "If you will wear this, all of my relatives who live along the way will know that you are a friend of mine. And if you should get into trouble they will help you in any way they can."

The toad wrapped the scarf tightly around his neck, and they bid each other farewell. With a quick push, off he went.

Swiftly he sped down the hillside, on and on, until he entered the dark woods at the edge of the valley. The little toad sailed between the trees, he darted under the bushes, he streaked past the rocks. Like a tiny rocket, he swept along the valley.

Just when he was almost through he noticed a dark shadow on the snow—a shadow that was racing right along beside him.

Nervously he looked up, hoping with all his heart that it wouldn't be what he knew it must be.

But it was. Gliding silently on broad wings, just above his head, the owl peered down at him through enormous yellow eyes. He seemed to float through the air with no effort at all.

The terrified toad could hardly take his eyes away. When he did, it was too late. A wall of old stones was suddenly in front of him. He tried to turn, but there was not enough time. Into the wall he crashed. He popped out of his skis and rolled and tumbled along the wall until he stopped in a heap.

When he brushed the snow from his eyes, the owl was standing on a log staring at him.

"Do I see a toad under all that clothing?" said the owl.

"Yes, you do," said Warton.

"In the middle of winter?"

"I'm going to visit my Aunt Toolia."

"Well, now you are going to visit me …" said the owl, "until next Tuesday, that is."

Warton tried to hop away, but one foot hurt so badly he couldn't move. The owl came closer, walking very slowly. Warton closed his eyes. As he did he thought he heard a whisper.

He looked around, only to see that the chill wind was
blowing small puffs of snow through holes in the stone wall,
and he knew that no one was there at all.

Then strong claws wrapped around him. He heard the
soft flapping of wings, and he felt the air of the deep woods
grow cold as he was lifted into the sky.

Studying the Selection

FIRST IMPRESSIONS

Would you leave your cozy home on a cold winter day to bring a treat through the ice and snow to your old aunt?

QUICK REVIEW

1. What was the argument between Warton and Morton about?

2. Morton gave two reasons that Warton should not go to visit Aunt Toolia at this time. What were they?

3. What ideas did Warton have to avoid any problems he might have on his trip?

4. What did the mouse give Warton as a gift?

FOCUS

5. What is one proof that Morton loved his brother, even though he argued with him?

6. Explain what the owl meant when he said, "Well, now you are going to visit me …"

CREATING AND WRITING

7. Beetle brittle must taste a lot like peanut brittle, which is a hard, flat piece of candy loaded with peanuts. Morton's beetle brittle was just delicious (if you are a toad, that is). When Morton packed up some to send to Aunt Toolia, he included the recipe. What do you suppose it was? On a piece of paper, list the ingredients and instructions for Morton's Beetle Brittle.

8. The story begins by telling us about two toads who live in a cozy home. Everyone has a different idea about what makes a home cozy. What is yours? Draw a picture of what you think is a cozy, comfortable room. Include the furniture, lighting, and objects that your room would have. At the bottom of the picture, write a sentence describing the weather outside.

PART TWO

Warton found himself being whisked over the tops of the trees. The evergreens below had the appearance of a thick carpet. The owl traveled fast and silently.

The winter sun was far down when Warton noticed that they were heading towards a particularly large spreading oak. The owl swooped through its snarly branches and into a hole near the top.

It was dark inside and smelled musty. The owl sat the toad in a corner and stepped back. He gave him a piercing look.

"What's your name?" he said.

"Warton."

"Warton?" said the owl. "Well, I think I'll call you … Warty."

"I don't care for that very much."

"You don't? Well, that's too bad … Warty!"

The little toad got up all his courage and looked right at the owl. "Are … are you going to eat me?"

The owl opened his yellow eyes wide. "Am I going to eat you? Of course I'm going to eat you!" Then the owl

walked across the room. On the wall a large calendar hung crookedly. The owl pointed at it. "Do you know what this says?"

The toad looked at it closely. "Yes, it says,

BERNIE'S GARAGE
Brakes and Front Ends Our Specialty"

"No! I don't mean that. You're not very bright, are you? It says that in five days it will be next Tuesday. And next Tuesday happens to be my birthday. And finding a little toad in the middle of winter is going to make me a special birthday treat. So, until that day, Warty, you may do as you please. From the looks of your foot I needn't worry about your trying to hop away. Besides, there is no way you can possibly get down from this tree."

The toad looked at his foot. It was twice its normal size. He gave a big sigh. Then he glanced around.

"Tell me, Warty," said the owl, "what do you think of my home?"

Warton looked around again, then he sniffed, then he blinked.

"Well?" said the owl.

"It's terrible," said the toad. "I would certainly hate to live here."

"Don't worry," said the owl, "you aren't going to for long."

"As long as I am here, I would like to make myself comfortable," said Warton. "Do you mind if I light some candles? It seems very dreary in here."

"Dreary?" said the owl. "It seems dreary? Well, go ahead if you want to. It doesn't matter to me."

The toad dug into his pack and pulled out two beeswax[1] candles. As soon as they were lit and began casting their warm glow about the room, he felt much better. He began to straighten his corner. And, being of a cheerful nature, he began to hum a little tune.

The owl couldn't believe his ears. "Warty, you did hear me say that I was going to eat you next Tuesday, didn't you?"

"Yes," said the toad.

The owl shook his head.

Warton continued to busy himself in his corner. Then he turned to the owl and said, "What's your name?"

---

1. While candles are made of various substances, such as tallow or paraffin, some are made of *beeswax* which, as its name says, is a wax produced by bees.

WORD BANK

dreary (DREER ee)
adj.: gloomy and sad

"I don't know," said the owl. "I guess I don't have one."

"What do your friends call you?"

"I don't have any friends."

"That's too bad," said Warton.

"No, it isn't too bad," snapped the owl. "Because I don't want any friends and I don't need any friends. Now, be quiet!"

Warton nodded. After a while he said, "If you did have a name, what would you like it to be?"

The owl began to be a little flustered. He wasn't used to talking to anyone, especially in his home. "Well, if I had a name …" he said slowly, "if I had a name … if I had a name … I think I would like … George."

"Uh huh," said the toad. He went back to straightening his corner.

The owl was becoming sleepy. He fluffed his feathers and closed his eyes.

Just as he was beginning to doze off, the toad called, "Hey, George!"

The owl's eyes popped open. "Are you talking to me?"

"Yes," said the toad. "Do you mind if I make some tea?"

"Oh, go ahead," said the flabbergasted owl.

Warton took some more things out of his pack and prepared the tea. While he waited for it to brew he slipped on his furry slippers and wrapped his favorite wooly bathrobe around himself. Shortly, he had a steaming pot of refreshing tea.

"It's ready, George," said the toad.

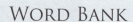

WORD BANK
flustered (FLUSS terd) *adj.*: nervous and confused
flabbergasted (FLAB er GASS ted) *adj.*: completely surprised
refreshing (rih FRESH ing) *adj.*: something that renews the energy of something else

"What's ready?" growled the sleepy owl.

"Our tea."

"I don't want any."

"But I've already got it poured," said Warton.

"Oh, all right," grumbled the owl.

Then, by the light of the beeswax candles, the owl and the toad sat down to tea.

"May I tell you something?" said Warton.

"What?" said the owl.

"When we were coming here today, even though I was scared as could be, I enjoyed going through the air like that. It must be wonderful to be able to fly wherever you want to."

"I guess it is," said the owl. Then he thought a bit. "Why yes, it is … it's just fine. I'll tell you, Warty, sometimes there's nothing I enjoy more than flying as high as I can and then just drifting along very slowly as I look down on everything. Although, that can be dangerous if you're not careful." He told the toad about a time when he was caught in the dark, rolling clouds of a thunderstorm. And how he was tossed about for hours amid hailstones and crackling streaks of lightning.

Warton was fascinated by the story. "Would you care for another cup of tea, George?"

The owl looked down at his empty cup. "I suppose I might as well," he said.

As Warton poured he said, "That's quite sly of you, George, flying about during the day like that when all other owls are sleeping."

"Is that so!" snorted the owl. "Well, it so happens that I just can't stay awake all night. The last time I tried I fell asleep on my way home, and I flew straight into the biggest beehive I ever saw in my life." The owl shuddered as he remembered that night.

Warton chuckled.

Then the owl talked further and the toad listened. Then the toad talked and the owl listened. It wasn't until the latest hours of that night when the owl finally said, "I'm too tired to talk any more." And he went to sleep.

Warton put away the teacups and then he put out the beeswax candles. As he lay in the still darkness he tried very hard to think of what he should do. But, because of the very busy day he had had and because of all the new experiences, his tired head just would not work at all. He was soon snoring softly.

When the toad awoke the next morning, the owl was gone. The swelling on Warton's foot had gone down but it was still quite sore. The sun shone in through the doorway, and in the bright light of day the owl's home did not seem nearly as gloomy as it had the night before. But it did look every bit as cluttered.

Warton poked through his pack trying to find something that would be just right for breakfast. He selected an ant-egg salad sandwich. As he unwrapped it his eyes turned to the wall opposite the doorway. A ray of sunlight fell directly on the owl's calendar. A large circle had been drawn around the day of his birthday, and an X put upon the day just past.

Only five days were left!

Warton's appetite nearly vanished, but he managed to eat his breakfast. When he was finished he went to the doorway and looked out.

The snow-covered ground was far, far below, and there was not a branch anywhere near that he could jump to. And even if he did somehow get down from the tree his foot was still too sore to travel on. "I shall just have to wait a bit," he thought.

All this time Warton had been studying the owl's home. Now something was bothering him almost as much as the coming of next Tuesday. That was the sorry state of the owl's housekeeping. Warton could stand it no longer.

Immediately he set about cleaning up the mess.

That was the reason he got along so well with his brother Morton. For, as much as Morton loved to cook, Warton loved to clean up messes. So their home was always neat and sparkling clean. The little toad just couldn't help himself. Before he knew it he was covered with dirt and dust as he hobbled about, being careful not to step too heavily on his sore foot.

All morning and all afternoon he cleaned. He didn't even stop for lunch. He had barely finished his work when he heard the soft flapping of wings.

The owl had returned a little earlier than usual. He had never thought of cleaning his home himself, so he was astonished at what he saw.

"It doesn't look too bad, Warty," he said. Then he puffed himself up, and his eyes opened wide. "But don't think I'm going to change my mind about next Tuesday."

"I didn't do it for that reason," said Warton. He went to his pack and took out a fresh washcloth. Then he washed off all the dirt and dust that had gotten on him during the day.

When he was done he unwrapped another of the sandwiches Morton had made for him, and quietly ate his supper.

All the while he was eating his sandwich the owl stared straight at him. And all the while he ate his dessert, the owl stared straight at him.

> ## WORD BANK
>
> **astonished** (uh STAHN isht)
> *adj.*: extremely surprised

When Warton swallowed the very last bite the owl said, "Are you going to make tea again tonight?"

"Perhaps I will," said Warton.

"Perhaps I will have some too," said the owl softly.

So that night the toad and the owl once again sat down to tea. And once again it was very late before they slept.

The following morning, when the toad awoke, the owl was gone as before. Warton's foot felt much better, so the first thing he did was to look at the calendar. "Only four more days—I must do something soon," he thought anxiously.

He went to the doorway and looked down—it was still just as far to the bottom of the tree. He tried calling to a sparrow, then a chickadee, then a nuthatch, but all the little birds knew the owl lived in that tree. None would come near.

Warton hopped all about, looking for some means of escape. He came upon a few of the owl's last year's feathers that he had somehow missed when he cleaned the owl's home.

"Maybe if I tie some of the feathers to my arms, I could glide to the ground," he thought. Then he laughed aloud at the silliness of the idea.

He decided to clean the owl's home again. When there was nothing left to clean, he ate his lunch. Then he did some jumping exercises to clear his head for serious thinking. When his head was clear, he squatted under the kitchen table and began to think.

First one eye blinked, then the other. Slowly, at first, then faster and faster he blinked, until everything became a blur. Then he stopped, smiling.

He hopped to the doorway again and looked down. "I think two and a half will do it," he said, hopping back to his corner. Opening his pack, he took out his three tightly-knitted sweaters. The blue one, the yellow one, and the white one with the red reindeer.

"There is more than enough strong yarn here to reach the bottom of this tree," he thought.

He began unraveling the blue sweater. And as he unraveled, he tied small loops in the yarn, just far enough apart for him to step into.

"This ladder is going to take me a couple of days," he thought, looking anxiously at the calendar. "And of course, I won't be so warm, and I won't have my skis, but at least I'll be free."

For the rest of the day he unraveled and made loops and hummed softly. When he thought it was almost time for the owl to come home he hid everything in his pack.

> ## WORD BANK
>
> **unraveled** (un RAV uld) *v.*: took apart threads, strings, yarn, or the like

It was none too soon, for the owl had returned even earlier than the day before. After supper the two had tea.

Drinking tea always put Warton into a mood for talking. And now that he knew he had a way of escaping he felt relaxed. Over their second cup of tea, he told the owl about the time he and Morton had come home from blueberry picking and found two snakes sleeping on their doorstep. He told how they had tied the snakes' tails together, hit them on their noses with the blueberry pails, then hopped off in different directions. When the snakes tried to catch them they became so snarled that Warton and Morton were able to roll them down the hill like a big ball, straight into the home of a cranky skunk.

The toad chuckled as he told the story. Then he noticed that the owl was laughing. "I'm glad you liked the story," said Warton.

"I didn't say that I liked it," snapped the owl.

"But you were laughing," said the toad.

"I was?" said the owl. "I don't believe I ever did that before."

As the toad filled their cups again, the owl said, "This is very good tea."

"Yes, it is," said Warton, "but not as good as my favorite of all teas."

"What is that?" asked the owl.

"Juniper-berry tea. My cousin once brought me some. I've never

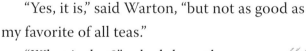

WORD BANK

snarled (SNAHRLD)
adj.: knotted; tangled up

tasted any as good. But it grows only in certain places and I've never had it again."

And they talked some more.

After Warton blew out the beeswax candles he said, "Goodnight, George."

There was a long, long silence. Then the owl said, "Goodnight, Warty."

The next day was just the same. In the morning when the toad awoke, the owl was gone. Warton worked on his unraveled-sweater-ladder until the owl returned. Later they drank some tea and had a chat.

On Sunday morning, even though his ladder wasn't finished, Warton decided to test it. He fastened one end to the owl's saggy sofa. The other end he dropped out of the doorway. Lying on his belly, he placed one foot over the edge and into the first loop. That one held.

He put his other foot into the next loop. That one held, too. Now he could see all the way to the ground, and it made him dizzy.

But Warton had to be sure that his ladder would really work. So down he went to another loop, another, and then another. Finally he was satisfied.

Climbing back up was much more difficult. Warton was all out of breath when he crawled into the owl's home. After a few minutes' rest he went back to work on his ladder. From time to time he glanced anxiously at George's clock. Because it had only the small hand it was very difficult to know exactly what time it was.

Finally, even though he had much more to do, Warton dared not work any longer. "Tomorrow I will have to work as fast as I can every possible minute if I am to finish in time," he thought. As he put the ladder in his pack another thought came to him, "Unless … unless George changes his mind. Then I won't need this ladder at all." Warton was thinking about how the owl came home earlier and earlier each day and how he seemed to enjoy their chats very much. At times he even seemed almost friendly. "Why, he may not eat me after all!" The thought suddenly made Warton feel quite happy.

But that day the owl returned home later than he had ever done before. It was almost dark when he stepped through the doorway.

Warton was still feeling quite happy. "Good evening, George," he said cheerily. "Did you have a nice day today?"

The owl stood staring down at the toad, his eyes cold as ice. "No …" he said slowly, "I did not have a nice day. I have been crunched up in a hollow log since early this morning. I did not catch the mouse that I chased in there, and when I started to come out, a fox was waiting at the entrance. He didn't leave until a short while ago. I have had nothing to eat all day. I am hungry and I am stiff and a storm must be coming because my talons are beginning to ache terribly."

Warton's happiness vanished instantly. He knew now that to depend upon the owl's having a change of heart could be a fatal

WORD BANK

talons (TA lunz) *n.*: claws of a bird

fatal (FAY tul) *adj.*: something that causes death

mistake. The ladder was his only hope, and yet there was so much more work to do and—the toad sighed—so little time.

It was not much later when the wind began howling through the dark woods and fine flakes of snow whipped through the branches of the oak. Indoors it was warm and cozy, and to take his mind off his misery Warton decided to play a game of solitaire. The owl was soaking his talons in a pan of hot water.

As Warton was getting out his deck of cards the owl noticed something else that he took out of his pack.

"What's in that white box, Warty?"

"Beetle brittle," said the toad.

"Perhaps I will have a piece," said the owl.

"Oh, I'm sorry," said Warton, "but this is for my Aunt Toolia."

Because of his aching talons, the owl was already in a bad mood. Now he became angry. "I only want one piece," he snapped. "And besides, what makes you think you are ever going to see your Aunt Toolia again?" He stepped out of the pan and snatched the box away.

Slowly, the owl ate one piece. "Hmmm, this is delicious."

"Of course," said Warton. "Everything my brother makes is delicious."

"Is that so," said the owl. "And I'll just bet your brother would be delicious too."

That made the toad angry.

The owl noticed it. "Oh, I ate only one piece," he grumbled. He closed the box and went to put it away in Warton's pack.

As he did his yellow eyes fell on Warton's ladder.

"Well …" he said as he pulled it out of the pack. "Well … Well … Well …" He walked to the doorway. "Well … Well … Well … Well …." And away went Warton's ladder into the howling wind.

The owl said no more that night.

Warton's heart became heavier than it had ever been in all his life. For the first time, there was absolutely no hope in it.

Studying the Selection

FIRST IMPRESSIONS
What do you think it feels like to fly through the air? What would the view be like?

QUICK REVIEW

1. What did the owl say he was going to do on Tuesday?
2. Why did the owl fly about during the day, when most owls only come out at night?
3. What was Warton's favorite pastime?
4. Why did Warton unravel his sweaters?

FOCUS

5. How does the owl change from the time Warton arrives until the end of Part Two?
6. Write down one line of dialogue in the story that tells the reader whether a character is nice or mean. Write down another line of dialogue that tells the reader about something that will happen in the plot. Make sure to put quotation marks around each line.

CREATING AND WRITING

7. Pretend that while Warton was the owl's prisoner, he kept a diary. Each night he would write down his thoughts and plans. What do you think he wrote? On a sheet of paper, write Friday, Saturday, Sunday, Monday, and Tuesday in a column. Between each day, leave a few lines. Then go back and write two sentences for each day's entry. Make sure your entries show that time is running out!

8. It is fun to have a class calendar. It would include your class' birthdays, holidays, and special event days. Your teacher will divide your class into groups and give each group two or three pages of a big calendar. The groups will mark all the special days that are on their calendar pages. They will decorate the dates and write what will take place on those dates. The teacher can then post all the pages on the bulletin board to form a one-year class calendar.

PART THREE

On the next night, the eve of the owl's birthday, neither one of them spoke at all. The owl just sat, and his great yellow eyes stared straight ahead. The little toad hummed no tune that night. It was still very early when he puffed out the beeswax candles.

For a long, long time he lay awake. He thought about many things—things he had done and things he had hoped to do. But mostly he thought about his brother. And he knew how much Morton would miss cooking special meals for him. He thought about their tidy home, and wondered if it would become messy. Finally, exhausted by hopelessness and sorrow, he fell into a deep sleep.

As on all other mornings, when Warton awoke the owl was gone. He washed up as always, but went without breakfast. The day before, he had eaten the last of Morton's lunches.

Sadly he looked at the calendar. There were no more days to be crossed off. This was the owl's birthday.

For a long time Warton sat staring at the calendar. Then, suddenly he heard a sound—a very distant sound. The owl was returning early for his birthday treat, he supposed. What would it be like? Warton wondered with a shudder.

Then he realized that the sound was not coming from outside the tree at all. He listened very carefully. At first it seemed to be coming from one of the dark corners of the room.

He hopped over. Now it seemed to come from within the heart of the tree itself.

Holding his breath, he went on listening. Whatever it was, it was coming closer. Could some other animal live in this tree—an animal that ate toads?

The sound grew louder. Warton could clearly hear the clicking of teeth and the scratching of sharp claws. He looked about for a place to hide, but it was too late.

On the wall, close to the floor, a hole was appearing. Quickly it grew a little larger, then out popped seven or eight delicate whiskers, followed by a tiny nose and furry body. And there, standing before Warton, was a brown and white mouse like the one that had given him the red scarf.

"Hi, I'm Sy," said the mouse, shaking sawdust from his whiskers.

The toad was overjoyed. "Hello, I'm Warton. I was afraid at first that you were the owl coming home early for his birthday treat, which is me. Then I was afraid that you were some other animal that lived in this tree and liked to eat toads. I've been quite nervous this past day or two."

"I don't blame you," said the mouse, "but don't worry, I and my brothers will help you escape."

"Oh, thank you," said Warton, "but how did you know I was here?"

"We were watching you as you traveled through the dark woods. We saw that you were wearing the special scarf. After you crashed into the wall, I whispered to you, but I don't think you heard me."

"I remember a kind of whispering," said Warton. "Was that you? I thought it was the wind."

"That was me all right," said Sy. "When the owl said he was going to take you home and save you for Tuesday, I knew we had a few days to think of a way to help you escape. But I didn't think it would take this long."

"That's all right," said Warton, "I have not been harmed."

"Great!" squeaked Sy, his eyes bright with excitement. "My brothers are waiting for us at the bottom of the tree. So, come! It's time to flee!"

Warton could see that Sy was enjoying the rescue immensely, but he wondered how much protection a few little mice would be.

WORD BANK

immensely (ih MENTS lee)
adv.: very, very much

Quickly, he threw his belongings into the pack. He knew he must leave as soon as possible, yet, when he picked up the beeswax candles he stood for a moment. He could not help but think fondly of the chats he and the owl had had over tea.

"Hurry! Hurry!" ordered Sy in his loudest squeak. "He may return at any moment."

Warton put the candles in the pack along with a scrap of paper that had been lying on the table. He could not leave the owl's home untidy.

Next, he put on every bit of his warm clothing—four coats, one-half of a tightly knit sweater, two pairs of mittens, and his cap with the ear flaps. Then he followed the mouse into the dark hole.

Beyond it was a narrow passageway, full of twists and turns. Some spots were so narrow the two could just barely squeeze through.

"We're going downward now," Sy said when they reached the center of the old tree. "Hold tightly to my tail or else you'll fall."

> **WORD BANK**
>
> **passageway** (PASS uj way)
> *n.*: a way that one passes
> through, such as a hall or alley

Halfway down they passed a small opening. Inside was a family of squirrels just sitting down to breakfast. Warton pictured Morton eating breakfast all alone, and felt homesick.

It was a long way down, but at last they reached the bottom of the giant tree. Blinking in the sunlight, Warton looked around him. Everything looked beautiful, and the crisp air made him feel good all over.

"Meet my brothers," said Sy proudly.

There, standing on skis exactly like Warton's and leaning on porcupine ski poles, were at least one hundred mice.

"When we saw how fast you traveled on those sticks of yours we decided to make some, too," Sy explained. "Of course, we brought yours along for you."

Warton was speechless. Never had he seen so many mice at one time, and all on skis.

"Let anyone try to stop us now!" shouted Sy. "Right, boys?"

"Right!" squeaked back a hundred voices.

"Then, let's go!" cried Sy.

Forming two long lines, with Warton and Sy in front, off they went. The hundred mice and one toad became a weaving ribbon that wound swiftly through the trees of the wooded valley. As they sped by, the other creatures of the woods stared in astonishment. Rabbits gawked, squirrels gaped, and birds gasped. No one had ever seen such a sight before.

As they zipped along, Warton said, "I never dreamed you had so many brothers, Sy."

WORD BANK
wooded (WOOD ed) *adj*.: having many trees
gaped (GAIPT) *v*.: stared at in wonder with an open mouth

"They're not even all here," said Sy. "Because of the accidents."

"Accidents?" said Warton.

"Yesterday, when we were trying our new skis for the first time, fourteen of my brothers ran into each other," Sy explained. "Seven turned their ankles, four banged their noses, and three backed into ski poles and won't be able to sit down for at least a week."

Then he began to sing a stirring marching song. The two brothers behind him joined in, then the next two, and the next, until the whole string of skiing mice were singing loudly as they whooshed along.

After they had gone some distance, they came to an open meadow on a hillside. At the bottom was an icy stream.

"We'll rest here a short time," said Sy. "When we're refreshed, we will finish our journey."

WORD BANK

stirring (STUR ing) *adj.*: arousing one's emotions

"Good," said Warton. "That will give me a chance to thank you and all your brothers—" He never finished, for something had caught his eye.

Down below, near the stream, some kind of struggle was going on. Puffs of snow flew in every direction. Even from such a distance, a great deal of screeching and growling could be heard. When the snow cleared away for an instant, Warton saw someone he thought he knew.

"George?" he said under his breath. Shading his eyes from the bright sun, he looked again.

He was right. George the owl was struggling frantically to free himself from the jaws of a snarling fox. Warton could see at once that George didn't have the slimmest chance.

Even now, the owl's wings were flapping weakly against the snow, while flying feathers filled the air.

Warton hopped to his feet and strapped on his skis.

"Where are you going?" asked Sy.

"I'm going to help George."

"George? Who's George?"

"George, the owl," said Warton.

"But … but … I thought we were helping you to get away from him," said Sy in bewilderment.

"Yes," said Warton, "but I just can't stand here and watch that fox eat him."

"But, he was going to eat *you*."

Warton wasn't listening. He pushed off toward the icy stream.

Sy scratched his head. "I never did understand toads. Well, come on, my brothers!" he squeaked with a twitch of his whiskers. "Let's give him a hand."

At once, all the mice jumped onto their skis and pushed off after Warton. The sunny hillside was one great wave of skiing mice as they flashed over the glistening snow. A powdery cloud rose high behind them as the one hundred mice and one toad swept downwards.

The fox looked up and blinked unbelievingly. Faster and faster they came, the sharp points of their poles glittering like diamonds and each one pointing straight at him. Quickly the fox decided that he wanted no part of whatever it was.

WORD BANK

bewilderment (bih WIL dur ment) *n.*: confusion

He released the owl, and bounded off through the deep snow as fast as his shaking legs would go.

The toad was the first to reach the owl. Most of the mice stopped a safe distance away, but Sy and a few of his brothers kept right after the terrified fox.

Warton looked sideways at the crumpled owl. Feathers were scattered all over the snow. Some floated slowly away in the icy stream. The owl's wings were badly tattered and one of his big yellow eyes was swollen completely shut.

As he looked at the once proud bird, Warton felt sad.

"Hello, Warty," said the owl weakly.

"Hello, George," said the toad.

"What are you doing here?" asked the owl.

"I'm escaping."

The owl's one good eye opened wide. "Escaping? Escaping from what?" he said, clearly annoyed.

"From you," said the toad. "Today is your birthday, and you said you were going to eat me. I was to be your special treat."

The owl started to shake his head, but it hurt too much. "Didn't you see my note?" he said, sounding more and more exasperated.

Then Warton remembered the piece of paper he had cleared from the table. "I—I didn't have time."

"Well, if you had, you would have known that I was coming home soon, and that I was going to bring a surprise."

"A surprise?" said Warton.

"That's what I said. I first came here to the stream to get a nice fish for supper, which I did. But, the surprise is over there, and that's where the fox caught me." The owl turned and pointed to some bluish-green bushes.

"Why, those are juniper bushes," said the toad.

"That's right," said the owl. "You said juniper berries made your favorite kind of tea, didn't you?"

Warton hardly knew what to say. "But I don't understand … do you mean you came here to pick them for me, and you weren't going to eat me, ever?"

"Of course I was going to eat you—until last night, that is." The owl spoke more softly. "Because we weren't speaking, I thought quite a bit last night. I thought about our chats and other things, and I thought that perhaps having a friend might not be too bad. I mean … I don't need any friends, of course … but …" As he spoke, two feathers fluttered to his feet. Then the owl turned his head so that Warton couldn't look at him. When he spoke again his voice was so soft the toad could barely hear him. "But if I ever do have a friend … I hope he is just like you … Warton."

Warton was stunned. From somewhere deep inside, a small lump had come into his throat. "Do you mean you would like us to be friends?" he said.

The owl nodded his head.

Then the toad hopped around to where he could look up at him. "I would be happy to be your friend, George."

The owl looked down and a big smile slowly spread across his battered face. "Well, that's fine. That's just fine. I'm so happy I promise I'll never eat another toad again." He looked around at Sy and his brothers, "Or a mouse, for that matter."

The mice cheered.

"Now, if I can still fly," he said, shaking out a few more loose feathers, "I'd be glad to take you the rest of the way to your Aunt Toolia's."

The toad hopped onto his back, shouting goodbye and thank you to Sy and to all his brothers. It took the owl some time to lift out of the snow, but finally he rose into the air. The higher he flew, the stronger he became. Warton waved

to the mice, as, far below, they grew smaller and smaller. Then the forest trees seemed to float beneath them as they made a great circle in the blue sky and turned towards Aunt Toolia's.

ABOUT THE AUTHOR

Russell E. Erickson grew up in Connecticut, and he still lives there today. He went through several different careers before turning to writing for children. Mr. Erickson enjoys fishing, vegetable gardening, hiking in the woods, and carpentry. He takes the nature descriptions in his books from his own fishing and camping experiences. When Mr. Erickson starts writing a story, he has no idea what is going to happen next. For him, part of the fun of writing is surprising himself while he is doing it!

ABOUT THE ILLUSTRATOR

Lawrence Di Fiori, often called "Larry," grew up in Pennsylvania, where his parents owned a restaurant. He has always worked in the art world. After studying art in college, he worked as an art teacher, illustrator, and puppet designer. He also served as an officer in the American Army. Larry Di Fiori has written and illustrated eleven of his own books, and he has illustrated more than fifty books written by others, including seven for the author of *A Toad for Tuesday*.

Studying the Selection

QUICK REVIEW

1. How did Sy know where to find Warton?

2. How did Sy and Warton get out of the owl's nest?

3. What was happening to George the owl just as Warton was escaping?

4. What surprise had George planned for Warton?

FOCUS

5. What was it that changed George's mind about eating Warton?

6. In the dialogue near the end of the story, Warton sums up how George now feels about him. Find that line of dialogue and write it down.

CREATING AND WRITING

7. The story ends with Warton on his way to see Aunt Toolia. Imagine the conversation he had with her when he arrived! Using the rules you have learned about writing dialogue, write down that conversation. Make sure you have Aunt Toolia speaking at least twice and Warton speaking at least twice.

8. You have now finished reading the book *A Toad for Tuesday*. Design a beautiful book jacket for the book. Your book jacket should have a picture on it that describes something in the story and that will make anyone who sees it want to read the book.

6 wrap-up
the grand finalé!

Activity One

Your teacher will divide the class into three groups. Each group will be assigned one of the three stories in Unit Six. The teacher will then distribute materials for making paper bag puppets. The members of each group will each choose one character from their story and create a puppet of that character. Make sure that there is a puppet of every character in your story, as it will be needed in Activity Three.

ACTIVITY TWO

Now is your chance to voice an opinion about any selection in the entire book! Choose one story that you either liked the most or liked the least. Write one paragraph explaining why you liked or disliked this selection and be prepared to read it to the class when your teacher calls on you.

Rocks in His Head

The Naming of Olga da Polga

A Toad for Tuesday

ACTIVITY THREE

For this activity, you will use the puppets you made for Activity One to put on a puppet show. Your teacher will give your group time to write down what your puppets will "say" and "do." When the shows are ready, the groups will take turns performing for the rest of the class.

Morton and Warton from *A Toad for Tuesday* had many adventures. Write your own Morton and Warton story. If you have time, you can even draw an illustration or two!

Activity Four

- GLOSSARY
- ACKNOWLEDGMENTS
- INDEX OF AUTHORS AND TITLES

glossary

A

addressed (uh DRESSD) *v.*: directed his words to

admiration (AD mih RAY shun) *n.*: respect and approval

astonished (uh STAHN isht) *adj.*: extremely surprised

awkwardly (AWK wurd lee) *adv.*: uneasily; uncomfortably

B

befitting (bih FIT ing) *adj.*: proper for; fitting

bewilderment (bih WIL dur ment) *n.*: confusion

bruised (BROOZED) *adj.*: slightly injured

burrowed (BURR ode) *v.*: living in a hole dug deep in the ground

C

captives (KAP tivs) *n.*: people that are captured

carousel (KER uh SEL) *n.*: a merry-go-round

cautiously (KAW shus lee) *adv.*: carefully and a bit anxiously

chaos (KAY ahss) *n.*: complete confusion

circumference (sur KUM fer unts) *n.*: the border of a circle

clattered (KLATT erd) *v.*: made a loud, rattling sound

coarse (KORSE) *adj.*: thick and rough

cobblestones (KAH bl STONES) *n.*: a naturally rounded stone that was used to pave streets

cocoon (kuh KOON) *n.*: a silky case in which certain insects enclose their eggs

confidence (KAHN fih DENTS) *n.*: belief in oneself

considered (kun SID erd) *adj.*: thought about

constant (KAHN stunt) *adj.*: continuing without a stop

converge (kuhn VURJ) *v.*: meet

countless (KOWNT less) *adj.*: a large number of something; too many to count

craving (KRAY ving) *n.*: a strong desire for something

crouched (KROWCHD) *v.*: stooped low to the ground

cyclone (SIKE lone) *n.*: a very strong storm in which the wind blows in a great circle

glossary

D

darted (DART ed) *v.*: started suddenly and ran swiftly

dazzled (DAZ uld) *v.*: overpowered by the brightness of something

debated (dih BAYT ed) *v.*: argued

declared (dih KLAIRD) *v.*: said firmly

define (dee FINE) *v.*: explain

delicacies (DEL ih kuh seez) *n.*: delicious food

descends (dih SENDS) *v.*: comes down

desperate (DESS prut) *adj.*: done because of tremendous need

disbelief (DIS bih LEEF) *n.*: not believing

disguise (dis GIZE) *v.*: to hide the way something looks

dismount (DIS mount) *v.*: to get off a horse

dodged (DOJD) *v.*: avoided by jumping aside

dreary (DREER ee) *adj.*: gloomy and sad

drought (DROWT) *n.*: a lack of rain

E

enormous (ih NORR muss) *adj.*: huge

etched (ETCHD) *v.*: sharply outlined

exasperated (ig ZASS per AYT ed) *adj.*: fed up; very annoyed

F

fatal (FAY tul) *adj.*: something that causes death

fertile (FUR tuhl) *adj.*: the type of soil or land in which plants grow easily

flabbergasted (FLAB er GASS ted) *adj.*: completely surprised

flickered (FLIK erd) *v.*: shone with a wavering light

flustered (FLUSS terd) *adj.*: nervous and confused

fringe (FRINJ) *v.*: to make a fringe, a border of loose threads at the end of a scarf or shawl

G

gaped (GAYPT) *v.*: stared at in wonder with an open mouth

garnets (GAR nets) *n.*: a semiprecious stone that is a deep red color

gawk (GAWK) *v.*: stare

glistened (GLISS und) *v.*: shone and sparkled

gnarled (NARLD) *adj.*: bent and twisted

glossary

gradually (GRAD ju uh lee) *adv.*: slowly but surely

gratitude (GRAT ih tood) *n.*: appreciation; thankfulness

H

hesitation (HEZ ih TAY shun) *n.*: a delay due to uncertainty or fear

hibernation (HI ber NAY shun) *n.*: the act of sleeping through the winter months

hues (HYUZE) *n.*: colors

I

immensely (ih MENTS lee) *adv.*: very, very much

inhabitants (in HAB ih tunts) *n.*: the people or animals who live in a place

insistently (in SIS tint lee) *adv.*: demanding a response

intent (in TENT) *adj.*: determined

J

jerky (JUR kee) *adj.*: sudden, sharp movements

K

kindhearted (KIND HART ed) *adj.*: good, generous, and kind

L

lift *n.*: a device found in mechanics' garages that can lift cars several feet off the ground

livestock (LIVE stock) *n.*: the horses, cattle, sheep, and other useful animals kept on a farm

M

merge (MURJ) *v.*: come together

mineralogist (MIN er AH luh jist) *n.*: a scientist who studies the group of rocks known as minerals

molasses (muh LASS us) *n.*: a thick, dark brown syrup produced when sugar is being refined

O

outwitted (out WIT ed) *v.*: outsmarted

P

passageway (PASS uj way) *n.*: a way that one passes through, such as a hall or alley

pleading (PLEED ing) *n.*: begging

produce (pro DOOS) *v.*: make

Q

quarries (KWAR eez) *n.*: pits that contain large amounts of stone that can be used for building

glossary

R

reassuring (REE uh SHUR ing) *adj.*: giving one confidence

refreshing (rih FRESH ing) *adj.*: something that renews the energy of something else

rigid (RIH jid) *adj.*: stiff and motionless

rivets (RIH vets) *n.*: metal pins that go through two or more pieces of metal, holding them together

rumbling (RUM bling) *n.*: a deep, continuous, low sound that is like a soft thunder

S

skimmed *v.*: passed over lightly

snarled (SNAHRLD) *adj.*: knotted; tangled up

snooze *n.*: a short nap

solemnly (SOLL uhm lee) *adv.*: seriously

somersaulted (SUM er SAWLT ed) *v.*: rolled head over heels

speculating (SPEK yoo LAYT ing) *v.*: giving possible reasons for something

sputtered (SPUH terd) *v.*: made explosive, popping sounds

stirring (STUR ing) *adj.*: arousing one's emotions

stockyards (STOCK yards) *n.*: a yard for livestock

sturdy (STUR dee) *adj.*: strong and not easily broken

sympathy (SIM puh thee) *n.*: the ability to share the sorrow of another person

T

talons (TA lunz) *n.*: claws of a bird

tattered (TAT urd) *adj.*: torn and ragged

telltale (TELL tale) *adj.*: something that *tells* (reveals) something that would not be known otherwise

temptingly (TEMPT ing lee) *adv.*: in a way that makes one want it

toil (TOYL) *n.*: hard work

tufts *n.*: a bunch of cottony or feathery material

U

unaccustomed (UN uh KUST umd) *adj.*: unusual

unraveled (un RAV uld) *v.*: took apart threads, strings, yarn, or the like

uselessness (YOOS less ness) *n.*: not serving any purpose; of no use

glossary

V

vanished (VAN ishd) *v.*: disappeared

vital (VIE tul) *adj.*: extremely important

W

wafted (WAHF ted) *v.*: floated through the air

weathered (WEH thurd) *adj.*: roughened by the weather

withdrawn (with DRAWN) *v.*: pulled back

wooded (WOOD ed) *adj.*: having many trees

Y

yearned (YURND) *v.*: wanted very, very much

acknowledgments

Illustrators

Sharon Bunting: Bear Mouse; Over in the Meadow

Remy Charlip: Harlequin and the Gift of Many Colors

Eva Clair: Patrick and the Great Molasses Explosion; A Gift for Tía Rosa; Claw Foot; Beatrice's Goat; Snail's Pace; The Grasshopper; Metaphor; Springtime

Lawrence Di Fiori: A Toad for Tuesday

Lydia Martin: The Naming of Olga da Polga

Wendell Minor: Heartland

David Small: The Gardener

Bear Mouse
"Bear Mouse" adapted from *Bear Mouse* by Berniece Freschet. Text copyright © 1973 by Berniece Freschet. Reprinted by permission of the author.

Beatrice's Goat
From **Beatrice's Goat** by Page McBrier. Text copyright © 2001 by Page McBrier. Reprinted with the permission of Atheneum Books for Young Readers, an imprint of Simon & Schuster Children's Publishing Division. All rights reserved.

Beauty
"Beauty" from I AM A PUEBLO INDIAN GIRL by E YEH SHURE. COPYRIGHT (C) 1936 BY WILLIAM MORROW & CO., INC., RENEWED 1967 BY LOUISE ABEITA CHIWIWI. Reprinted by permission of HarperCollins Publishers.

Claw Foot
"Claw Foot" by Evelyn Witter. Text copyright © 1976 by Lerner Publications Company. Reprinted with the permission of Lerner Publications Company, a division of Lerner Publishing Group, Inc. All rights reserved. No part of this text excerpt may be used or reproduced in any manner whatsoever without the prior written permission of Lerner Publishing Group, Inc.

The Gardener
From THE GARDENER. Text Copyright 1997 by Sarah Stewart. Illustrations Copyright 1997 by David Small. Reprinted by permission from Farrar, Straus, Giroux Books for Young Readers. All Rights Reserved.

A Gift for Tía Rosa
A Gift for Tía Rosa by Karen T. Taha. Text © 1986 by Dillon Press, Inc. Reprinted by permission of the author in loving memory of Frances Carver, Aunt Fran.

The Grasshopper
From FAR AND FEW by David McCord. Copyright © 1952 by David McCord. By permission of Little, Brown and Company. All rights reserved.

Harlequin and the Gift of Many Colors
Harlequin and the Gift of Many Colors by Remy Charlip and Burton Supree. Copyright © 1973 by Remy Charlip and Burton Supree. Reprinted with the permission of The Wylie Agency.

Heartland
Copyright © 1989. Reprinted by permission of S©ott Treimel NY. Illustrations © 1989 by Wendell Minor.

Metaphor
From IT DOESN'T ALWAYS HAVE TO RHYME by Eve Merriam. C Renewed 1992. All Rights Reserved. Used by permission of Marian Reiner.

The Naming of Olga da Polga
From **The Tales of Olga da Polga** by Michael Bond. Text copyright © 1971 by Michael Bond. Reprinted with the permission of Simon & Schuster Books for Young Readers, an imprint of Simon & Schuster Children's Publishing Division. All rights reserved.

No Laughing Matter
No Laughing Matter © 2018 by Abigail Rozen. Printed by permission of the author.

Patrick and the Great Molasses Explosion
"Patrick and the Great Molasses Explosion" by Marjorie Stover, reprinted by permission of Charry Stover.

People
"People" from ALL THAT SUNLIGHT by Charlotte Zolotow. (c) 1967, renewed 1995 Charlotte Zolotow Trust. By permission of Edite Kroll Literary Agency, Inc.

Rocks in His Head
TEXT COPYRIGHT (c) 2001 BY CAROL OTIS HURST. Used by permission of HarperCollins Publishers.

Snail's Pace
From ALWAYS WONDERING Some Favorite Poems of Aileen Fisher. All Rights Renewed and Reserved. Used by permission of Marian Reiner on behalf of the Boulder Public Library, Inc.

Springtime
From *SPIN A SOFT BLACK SONG: POEMS FOR CHILDREN* © 1987 by Nikki Giovanni. Reprinted by permission of Farrar, Straus, Giroux Books for Young Readers. All Rights Reserved.

A Toad for Tuesday
A Toad for Tuesday written by Russell E. Erickson and illustrated by Lawrence Di Fiori. Text copyright © 1974 by Russell E. Erickson. Reprinted by permission of The Stuart M. Miller Co.

The Town That Moved
The Town That Moved by Mary Jane Finsand. Copyright © 1983 by Carolrhoda Books, Inc. Reprinted with the permission of Lerner Publishing Group, Inc. All rights reserved. No part of this text excerpt may be used or reproduced in any manner whatsoever without the prior written permission of Lerner Publishing Group, Inc.

Note: We have expended much effort to contact all copyright holders to receive permission to reprint their works. We will correct any omissions brought to our attention in future editions.

index of authors and titles

Italics indicates selection.

Roman indicates author biographical information.